T0381176

ONE VOICE

How the modern church has
turned from the voice of God

THOMAS QUINN KELLER

WestBow
P R E S S®
A DIVISION OF THOMAS NELSON
& ZONDERVAN

This book is a work of non-fiction. Unless otherwise noted, the
author and the publisher make no explicit guarantees as to the
accuracy of the information contained in this book and in some cases,
names of people and places have been altered to protect their privacy.

WestBow Press books may be ordered through
booksellers or by contacting:

WestBow Press
A Division of Thomas Nelson & Zondervan
1663 Liberty Drive
Bloomington, IN 47403
www.westbowpress.com
844-714-3454

Because of the dynamic nature of the Internet, any web
addresses or links contained in this book may have changed
since publication and may no longer be valid. The views
expressed in this work are solely those of the author and do
not necessarily reflect the views of the publisher, and the
publisher hereby disclaims any responsibility for them.

Any people depicted in stock imagery provided by Getty Images are
models, and such images are being used for illustrative purposes only.
Certain stock imagery © Getty Images.

ISBN: 979-8-3850-3010-1 (sc)
ISBN: 979-8-3850-3011-8 (e)

Library of Congress Control Number: 2024915097

Print information available on the last page.

WestBow Press rev. date: 11/06/2024

A WAKE-UP CALL

Hebrews 8:8-11 reads:

"Behold, days are coming, says the Lord, when I will bring about a new covenant with the house of Israel and the house of Judah—not like the covenant I made with their fathers on the day I took them by the hand to bring them out of the land of Egypt. For they did not continue in My covenant, and I did not care about them, says the Lord. For this is the covenant I will make with the house of Israel after those days, declares the Lord: I will put My laws into their minds and write them on their hearts. I will be their God, and they will be My people. And they will not teach, each one his fellow citizen and each one his brother, saying, 'Know the Lord,' for they will all know Me, from the least to the greatest of them. For I will be merciful toward their wrongdoings, and their sins I will no longer remember." (NASB)

I've got good news! This New Testament passage is no longer a prophecy. The writer of Hebrews is actually quoting Jeremiah's prophecy from hundreds of years earlier—and telling us that the age of this new covenant has *now* come! This longed-for age, when God would

1

place His laws directly in our hearts and minds, without the need for prophets or priests to guide us, has arrived! Isn't that incredible? And yet, tens of millions of Christians today are still waiting for this day to come. Christian, you've missed it!

"Missed it? How?" you might ask. "When? I'm a believer, part of the new covenant. This hasn't happened yet—or surely I would have experienced it. But I haven't, and neither has anyone I know." And therein lies the problem. You, your friends, family members, pastors, and Christian authors have all read something into God's Word that isn't there. You've made an assumption and then built your understanding of God on that faulty assumption. Just like the Jews of today who are still waiting for their Messiah, you're looking forward to a moment or an event that you'll never see—because you're looking past it. In this book, I'll aim to enlighten you, making the case that many problems in the church stem from this very misunderstanding. But before we dive into the details, let me pose a scenario to you.

I know it may never have occurred to you, but what do you think someone would believe if their only knowledge of God and the Christian faith came directly from God, without any outside influence? What would their faith look like today? Would it differ from yours? Do you believe your Christian faith, as you understand it, is exactly how God would have conveyed it to you if He were the only one teaching you? Is everything you believe about your faith scripturally accurate? And how do you know?

What if a dozen people were given the written Word of God and told to go off by themselves for three years, learning only from what they could gather from reading the Scriptures—nothing more? No outside influence, no pre-existing biases, no commentaries—just a person and their Bible. What conclusions would each of them come to? Wouldn't it be fascinating to find out? Do you think this has ever been done? Think about that for a moment before moving on. I'll wait...

"Now we have received, not the spirit of the world, but the Spirit who is from God, so that we might understand the things freely given us by God. And we impart this in words taught by the Spirit, interpreting spiritual truths to those who are spiritual. The natural person does not accept the things of the Spirit of God, for they are foolishness to him, and he is not able to understand them because they are spiritually discerned." (1 Corinthians 2:12-16, NKJV)

Okay, here's what I believe: If we picked 12 random people, it's quite possible they'd end up all over the place after three years, each with different ideas about what it means to be Christian. Why? Because for most people, God has hidden His understanding from them. They can't come to the truth—ever, not in their current state. Agreed? Jesus, God incarnate, delivered a simple message in the flesh, yet few understood Him. So we can't say, "If Jesus were here today, He would set things straight." He already came, and we've been there, done that.

"He answered and said to them, 'Because it has been given to you to know the mysteries of the kingdom of heaven, but to them

it has not been given. For whoever has, to him more will be given, and he will have abundance; but whoever does not have, even what he has will be taken away from him.'" (Matthew 13:11-12, NKJV)

This passage refers to spiritual understanding, not material gain. For many, God has closed their ears, blinded their eyes, and clouded their minds—for reasons we may never fully understand.

Now, let's change the scenario slightly but significantly. What if we found 12 people filled with the Holy Spirit of God (if we could somehow know for sure), gave them a Bible, and told them to do the same thing? What would happen then? I believe they would come to the same truth about God. They would understand what it truly means to be Christian and agree with one another. Why do I think this? Because it has already happened before. We have a case study: the apostles. They were taught by Christ alone during their first three years as Christians. Paul also spent his first three years with Christ and the Holy Spirit before consulting the apostles who preceded him. They all agreed on the gospel and its meaning for us as believers. The apostles and prophets were united in faith. None of the Scriptures contradict one another, even though they were written by 40 different men over 1,500 years.

Why don't we have unity in the faith today? There are two reasons, as I see it. First, I believe the problem lies in the fact that most professing Christians—around 2.5 billion people—are not truly born again of the Holy

Spirit. Second, those who are genuinely born again are influenced by a thousand voices, with God being just one of them.

That was me. I was a Christian just like many evangelical Christians in the U.S. I said the sinner's prayer, attended non-denominational churches, listened to Christian contemporary music, wore Christian T-shirts, voted Republican, and proudly identified as an American. I sent my kids to Christian schools, listened to everyone on the Salem Radio Network, watched Fox News, carried a sidearm, and drove an SUV. But then I made one change in my life, and within three years, none of those things mattered anymore. In fact, much of what I thought it meant to be Christian—and much of what the modern church teaches as doctrine—I came to believe is largely wrong.

You see, after over 30 years of being a Christian, I did something I had never done before: I picked up my Bible and read it—all of it.

Through a series of difficult circumstances, I decided to tune out all the noise and listen to Christ Himself. What does it mean to be a Christian in God's eyes? I needed to know, once and for all. What does He say about why I'm here, and what is required, if anything? How does He say I should live this Christian life? So, I opened my Bible to Genesis and began reading, praying that God would reveal His truth to me in the midst of the distractions, and I trusted that He would. This wasn't a chore—it was a quest!

Within a few months, I had read through the entire Bible. Within a year, I had finished my third reading. I started with a 1972 edition of the NIV. Then, I read the NKJV several times before moving on to the ESV, NASB, and even the lesser-known KJ3 Bible. I've enjoyed them all. These days, I've read through the Bible many times, and each time it speaks to me anew.

Why read more than one translation? Over-familiarity with a single translation can cause us to miss key details. I've found that switching translations helps me read with fresh eyes. This, I believe, is one of the keys to keeping Scripture alive and new. Looking at the Word with fresh eyes is essential if we are going to mature in our faith. Sure, some translations might differ in certain passages, but I firmly believe the truth can still be known through each one if read from beginning to end. It's my opinion that many Christians would benefit from reading Scripture in this way.

What I came to realize after my first three years of studying the Word—and what I am even more convinced of now—is that the church has strayed far from the tenets and true teachings of the Bible. Believing themselves to have become more enlightened in modern times, they have turned to myths instead. As I mentioned earlier, it's my strong belief that most professing Christians are not filled with the Holy Spirit of God. That applies to many, if not most, Christian leaders as well. If that's the case, then both they and their leaders are incapable of understanding Scripture correctly. While claiming to believe that the

Bible is God's Word, they unapologetically pick and choose which parts to accept, discarding the passages they don't like. Oh, most won't won't openly reject sections of Scripture—they just won't teach them. Worse yet, they'll twist them to fit their own theology.

Paul refers to anyone not filled with the Holy Spirit as a "natural man." The natural man—whether Christian or not—will struggle because God's Word is foreign to him. Without the Spirit, he has no choice but to come to erroneous conclusions about God and His teachings, even when some of those teachings are straightforward. The natural man prefers to create a god in his own image, from his own imagination, and doesn't mind what name this god goes by—even if it's the name "Jesus." This has always been the case.

I once debated a woman about the teachings of Joyce Meyer. After I quoted some of the things Meyer had said—things that were clearly made up and untrue—the woman responded, "Anyone who points to Jesus is okay with me." But what if it's the wrong Jesus? No, it's not okay! The Christian church as a whole believes in too many versions of Jesus! With these multiple "Jesuses" come multiple understandings of salvation, yet each group claims their understanding comes from God, when in reality, it's influenced by the writings of others. Many people also bring their own preconceived ideas and biases to the faith, imagining God the way they think He should be. This is why we have so many denominations: Catholic, Lutheran, Baptist, Presbyterian, Assemblies of God, Episcopal, Pentecostal, Evangelical, Methodist, Word of Faith, conservative, liberal—the list goes on. Is God really this confusing? How can so many people arrive at so many opposing conclusions if they are all filled with the same Holy Spirit? The answer is simple: they couldn't—at least not if they were only listening to Him and no one else. The real problem is all the other voices Christians choose to listen to. But in reality, there's only *one* voice, and that voice spoke through 40 select men—none of whom have been alive for over 2,000 years.

"We (the apostles and prophets exclusively) *speak the wisdom of God in a mystery—the hidden wisdom that God ordained before the ages for our glory, which none of the rulers of this age knew... But God has revealed them to us* (these same men) *through His Spirit. For the Spirit searches all things, yes, the deep things of God. For what man knows the things of a man except the spirit of the man which is in him? Even so, no one knows the things of God except the Spirit of God. Now we have received, not the spirit of the world, but the Spirit who is from God, so that we might know the things that have been freely given to us by God. These things we also speak,* **not in words which man's wisdom teaches** *but which the Holy Spirit teaches, comparing spiritual things with spiritual. But the natural man does not receive the things of the Spirit of God, for they* (spiritual truths) *are foolishness to him;* **nor can he know them, because they are spiritually discerned."** (1 Corinthians 2:7-14, NKJV, fragmented)

This is why the unspiritual man, even if he professes the same faith in Christ as the spiritual man, can believe so many opposing or different things about Christ and His way—and then turn around and teach those things to others. They are trying to interpret and understand Holy Scripture without the Holy Spirit, but that can't be done. And so, for 2,000 years, we've seen sheep acting like sheep, shepherds acting like wolves, and the Holy Spirit not acting at all.

And what about true spiritual believers? How have they gotten so much wrong? Well, that brings me to this book—an explanation of what I believe to be the largest contributor to the falling away of God's people from His Word, resulting in a gross misunderstanding of His gospel and our responsibility to it.

Throughout the history of the Bible, the majority of God's people have repeatedly gotten it wrong—from king to prophet to shepherd to sheep. This has always been the case, and things didn't change after Christ's resurrection and ascension.

"What has been will be again, what has been done will be done again; there is nothing new under the sun." (Ecclesiastes 1:9, NIV)

One of the biggest reasons for this gross misunderstanding of Scripture is that God's children have been conditioned to trust the words of man over the words of God. This isn't new. A simple reading of the Bible will prove that to be the case. The stories we read, the lives written about, are absolutely recorded as warnings for us believers today.

"Now these things took place as examples for us (modern-day Christians), *so that we might not desire evil as they did. Do not be idolaters, as some of them were; as it is written, 'The people sat down to eat and drink and rose up to play'* (this is a picture of what it is to idolize the world). *We must not indulge in sexual immorality, as some of them did, and 23,000 fell in a single day. We must not put Christ to the test, as some of them did and were destroyed by serpents, nor grumble, as some of them did and were destroyed by the Destroyer. Now these things happened to them as an example,* **but they were written down for our instruction,** *on whom the end of the ages has come. Therefore, let anyone who thinks that he stands* **take heed lest he fall.**" (1 Corinthians 10:6-12, ESV)

The warnings are clear. But if the church doesn't believe these warnings are for us—even when the New Testament writers say they are—then we will not heed them. Instead, we'll dismiss them as relics of the past. This has always been the pattern with God's people, and it will continue until Christ's second coming.

Those who dare to call attention to this pattern will be ridiculed and vilified, as has always been the case. The church prefers to say, "Peace! Peace!" as if they have peace with God, when in reality, they do not. So, I present this book as a wake-up call, knowing that I will likely be ignored at best and possibly hated by many. It is not my intent to offend, but rather to wake up a sleeping church. What follows is my attempt at a cold-water splash to the face. Wake up!

NOTE (For All of My Books)

My primary goal is to live a life that pleases God. I do not wish to lead anyone astray with this book, nor do I wish that for myself. I am deeply concerned, however, that God's teachings are being diluted by the very shepherds people look to for guidance. This has been the norm throughout the history of God's shepherds, and I firmly believe it continues today.

I must admit, I am likely to get off track (if I haven't already). It's a family trait—we're known for our tangents. Books need chapter titles, I suppose, so I have them, but I don't always stick to the topic. Please bear with me. By the end, I will get to where I'm trying to go. If you stick with me, we'll get there together. Yes, I repeat myself often, but so does God. Scripture makes the same points over and over again, to ingrain them in our consciences, and hopefully into our hearts and souls. There aren't that many themes running through the Bible. I'll touch on a few of them in this book.

Also, I know I tend to highlight words to emphasize a point, and I apologize if that gets annoying. Any commentary or words in parentheses within Bible passages that are not in italics are my own interjections, not part of the biblical text. In some longer passages, I may skip verses for brevity (noted by ...), but I am not trying to take Scripture out of context. If something seems off, I encourage you to read the full passage or chapter for yourself. God instructs us to test all teachings, and that includes mine.

Finally, I confess upfront that I may come across as inconsistent, or even hypocritical, in writing this book. I criticize shepherds, authors, and commentaries, yet I myself teach a small group bible study and I have written this book to you. If I'm being honest (and I am), I want you to read my books—and then be done reading books on faith or self-help. Of course, I'm not against all books. Enjoy your fiction, learn home improvement, or pick up a second language. But when it comes to knowing God, rely on His Word alone.

Lastly, my style is bold and direct. It's not a personal attack. It's a conscious tactic to ensure I'm not misunderstood. I won't soften the blows to spare feelings; my goal is not to offend but to save souls. When I say "you" instead of "we" or "they," I'm trying to get you to reflect on yourself, not think about others who might fit the descriptions I give. This book is for you, the reader.

Onward!

THE MANY FALSE SHEPHERDS

"His watchmen are blind;
they are all ignorant;
they are all dumb dogs,
they cannot bark;
sleeping, lying down, loving to slumber.
Yes, they are greedy dogs,
which never have enough.
And they are shepherds who cannot understand;
they all look to their own way,
every one for his own gain."
(Isaiah 56:10-11, NKJV)

I hesitated writing this chapter, knowing it wouldn't go over well. Church growth, the Christian speaking circuit, and the book industry rake in multi-millions of dollars a year. None of these promote the idea that God alone can lead His sheep, for obvious reasons. One night, shortly after finishing this chapter, I lay in bed wondering if I had gone too far. Was it too harsh? Concerned, I brought it before the Lord in prayer and eventually drifted off to sleep.

The next morning, as part of my daily routine, I woke up, walked into my study, sat down, and opened my Bible to where I had left off the night before. It turns out I had finished Isaiah 57 the night before. That morning, I began chapter 58:

"Cry aloud, do not hold back;
raise your voice like a trumpet,
and declare to my people their transgression
and to the house of Jacob their sins."
(Isaiah 58:1, ESV)

Coincidence or God? Just like that, my decision was made.

I was once on Facebook calling out my Christian friends on a wrong I saw in the church from Scripture. The response I got was, "You do you!" That might have been my last post on social media. The Bible clearly teaches that if we, God's children, see any of our brothers or sisters in Christ living contrary to Him, we are to call their attention to it and rebuke them. This is a biblical mandate, not an option. If, after being obedient to call it out, those rebuked continue in the wrong, that's on them. We are to "shake off the dust from that city and move on." However, if we keep quiet, their sin becomes ours as well.

Here's the principle:

*"When I say to the wicked, 'You shall surely die,' and you give him no warning, nor speak to warn the wicked from his wicked way, to save his life, that same wicked man shall die in his iniquity; **but his blood I will require at your hand.** Yet, if*

*you warn the wicked, and he does not turn from his wickedness, nor from his wicked way, he shall die in his iniquity; **but you have delivered your soul**."*
(Ezekiel 3:18-19, ESV)

*"Again, if a righteous person turns from his righteousness and commits injustice, and I lay a stumbling block before him, he shall die. **Because you have not warned him**, he shall die for his sin, and his righteous deeds that he has done shall not be remembered, but his blood I will require at your hand. **But if you warn the righteous person not to sin, and he does not sin,** he shall surely live because he took warning, and **you will have delivered your soul**."*
(Ezekiel 3:20-21, ESV)

That's how it works. For the Christian, since we are one body, "You do you, I'll do me" doesn't cut it. God is not fine with His children accepting sin in their lives or in the lives of their Christian siblings. As part of the family of God, we are here to lift up, admonish, encourage, and rebuke—not the world—but those who declare themselves citizens of God's kingdom. Cancer spreads and takes over the body if we don't rid ourselves of it, as God has called us to do.

So, what are the wrongs of our shepherds? In the beginning, God delegated to His prophets the task of leading His people verbally and by example, living a life of righteousness. He gave the world Abel, Enoch, Noah, Lot, and Abraham, yet the people listened to and behaved like everyone but them. It's why we got the flood and a firestorm, remember? Even after God gave us Moses, the people rarely chose to be led by true men appointed by Him.

Read the Isaiah passage again. It was the unholy, the unrighteous, the self-absorbed, and those without true understanding from the Lord who led the people—and all in the name of God. In His own words, God refers to the shepherds of His people (priests and prophets) as "dogs." Dogs! God does not pull punches. He's not here to play nice; He's here to be obeyed.

Throughout Scripture, the Lord routinely takes most priests, prophets, and would-be apostles to task for abusing their power, sleeping on the job, and leading His sheep astray. God put them in charge of teaching His people His laws and being examples for them to follow, with the express purpose of bringing His people into a life of obedience. Nothing has changed. This is what it means to be separate from the world. The world lives in darkness, but we, the people of God, are to live in the light. The overseers have sorely neglected the job God required of them.

But putting men in charge of God's message for the long term didn't work. Too many were fakes, professing to speak for God but speaking from their own minds, understanding, and wisdom. Enter the written Word.

Starting with Moses, God no longer relied on oral tradition to pass down His story and message. He recorded it in the written Word, specifically for us who would come later, so that the original intent would remain forever. This way the message couldn't be changed based on human sensibilities or societal norms from one generation or region to the next. Scripture is clear: God is not a fan of tradition, even church tradition.

As told by the Holy Spirit, Moses wrote about the beginning of the material world, mankind, and the events and people that followed, right through to most of his own life. Then, through 39 other men, God continued to reveal His plan, His holy character, His laws, and humanity's responsibility to them. This continued until His last epistle was written. Now we have God's Word, complete, just as He always intended. Everything He requires us to know has been written down and preserved for His people. And God says that His Word alone is everything we need to know about Him and how to walk with Him. Thus, the canonization of God's Word is the fulfillment of the prophecy in Jeremiah: "I will put my laws into their hearts and minds."

*"All Scripture is given by inspiration of God, and is profitable for doctrine, for reproof, for correction, for instruction in righteousness, **so that the man of God may be complete**, thoroughly equipped for every good work."*
(2 Timothy 3:16-17, NKJV)

Scripture is the written Word of God. It is the culmination of more than 1,500 years of God's perfect work, and I'm pretty sure He believes He has produced quite a good book. He likely doesn't think He left anything out. Yet many shepherds seem to believe there's more that needs to be included (Bible commentaries and book introductions come to mind). At the same time, much of what He *did* include is treated as unimportant by many in the church. It's as if God didn't mean for 75% of His work to be known by all men—as if the entirety of Scripture wasn't always His plan.

The church has rewritten God's Word through commentaries, and what we're left with is a religious facade fashioned to make Christianity more acceptable to the masses—the masses who willingly pay the bills. According to a report from the World Economic Forum (January 5, 2017), religious congregations in the U.S. alone take in $418 billion annually. Universities, charities, and health systems receive $303 billion, while faith-related businesses take in $437 billion. And I'm sure these numbers have increased since then.

Over and over in Scripture, we're warned about the lure of riches and the desire to be esteemed by others. Shepherds, dating as far back as the time of Judges, often chose personal gain over obedience to their role. Today's "shepherds" and influencers are often doing the same. If today's shepherds have been tasked with teaching the Word of God accurately and ensuring that the sheep adhere to it, they have failed miserably. Their bad teachings have become permission to allow sin into our lives. In fact, instead of teaching the truths of Scripture, many of God's shepherds today teach that it is impossible to adhere to God's Word.

The Bible is no longer considered the sole authority for the church. Instead, many pastors and theologians view it as just one of many important sources for understanding God. And in many cases, the local church is placed on equal footing with the Word of God. It's no wonder. If people don't want to understand what God is saying directly through Scripture, they'll turn to others to explain it—whether it's a church, a book, a speaker, or something else. This has always been the case, and therein lies the problem.

*"**I** have not sent these prophets, yet they ran. **I have not spoken to them, yet they prophesied.** But if they had stood in My counsel, and had caused My people to hear My words, **then they would have turned them from their evil way and from the evil of their doings**... Therefore behold, I am against the prophets,"* says the Lord, *"**who steal My words every one from his neighbor.** Behold, I am against the prophets,"* says the Lord, *"**who use their tongues and say, 'He says.'** Behold, I am against those who prophesy false dreams,"* says the Lord, *"and tell them, and cause My people to err by their lies and by their recklessness. Yet I did not send them or command them; **therefore they shall not profit this people at all,**"* says the Lord.* (Jeremiah 23:21-22, 30-32, NKJV)

It does not profit God's people to listen to these shepherds. They are no better off spiritually by having them around because the concepts and precepts they teach are wrong. But, in truth, the sheep like it that way. Remember—and this is critical—the Word of God is living! It speaks as much to us today as it did in any era, by design! Don't make the mistake of thinking, "That was then; this is now."

*"An astonishing and horrible thing has been committed in the land: **The prophets prophesy falsely,** and the priests* (pastors and priests) **rule by their own power**; *and My people* (the church as a whole) *love to have it so. But what will you do in the end?"*
(Jeremiah 5:30-32, NKJV)

The grave misunderstanding today is that Christians believe these warnings no longer apply now that Christ has come. Christian, this will always be an issue. Look at the immorality in the church today. The Word of God is true for every generation. It's why we still have it. It's not just a history lesson; it's a warning! The Word, along with the Holy Spirit, is God's only voice remaining for our faith. But too many choose to follow a faith handed down to them by others.

*"For false christs and false prophets will rise and show great signs and wonders to deceive, if possible, **even the elect.**"*
(Matthew 24:24, NKJV)

When were you thinking this was going to take place? As it was foretold in Old Testament times, so it was in the New Testament, and so it will continue.

*"And the Lord said to me, 'The prophets prophesy lies **in My name**. I have **not** sent them, commanded them, **nor spoken to them**; they prophesy to you a false vision, divination, **a worthless thing**, and the deceit of their heart. Therefore thus says the Lord concerning the prophets who prophesy in My name, **whom I did not send**, and who say, "Sword and famine shall*

not be in this land"—**by sword and famine those prophets shall be consumed!"'**
(Jeremiah 14:14-15, NKJV)

The text infers that God is referring to the majority of those professing to speak for Him, not the minority.

*"Beware of false prophets, who come to you **in sheep's clothing**, but inwardly they are ravenous wolves."*
(Matthew 7:15, NKJV)

"But what I do, I will also continue to do, that I may cut off the opportunity from those who desire an opportunity to be regarded just as we are (the authority of the apostles) *in the things of which they boast. For such are false apostles, deceitful workers, **transforming themselves into apostles of Christ**. And no wonder! For Satan himself transforms himself into an angel of light."*
(2 Corinthians 11:12-13, NKJV)

For some reason, today's Christians have come to believe that these warnings are about a few pastors on the fringe of the Christian church, as if Scripture is warning us about a few bad apples. Yet, the truth is, there have always been just a few *good* apples. Read your Bible! It's the good apples that have always been the exception, not the bad ones. There are many priests, pastors, and ministers today who have convinced themselves—and their followers—that they are modern-day apostles, warning or belittling sheep who dare to reach different conclusions. These shepherds are treated as celebrities, just like the Jewish priests of old. And they love it. Too often, they are blindly followed and unquestioned by "the many." But nice people can be very wrong and spread lies, whether intentional or not. This is still happening today. They don't come across as evil or liars; they appear as angels of light! Don't you get it?

Many shepherds even consider themselves to have the same authority as the apostles, as if this authority has been passed down to them from the original apostles. It hasn't. The apostles of Scripture were uniquely tasked to finish the ministry Jesus gave them. That ministry, I believe, ended when the last epistle was written and the apostles' lives came to an end.

Paul warned about "influencers" in the church:

*"**For many walk**, of whom I have told you **often**, and now tell you even weeping, **that they are the enemies of the cross of Christ:** whose end is destruction, whose god is their belly, and whose glory is in their shame—who set their mind on earthly things."*
(Philippians 3:18-19, NKJV)

Yes, these are today's wolves in sheep's clothing. Proving themselves to be enemies of the cross, they come as "angels of light." Meaning, they are easy to like and follow! God has not sent them—man has, and church tradition has. Whether they have been placed into authority or have placed themselves there, their followers wrongly recognize them as authoritative. Listen: no one has spiritual authority over a believer's life but the Word of God. Yet, church traditions, conceived by men, have been endorsed as important practices within the body of Christ.

Church tradition has been given too much authority in the church—so much so that these traditions have come to be thought of as the very mandates of God. Man-made "institutions of higher learning" come to mind. These human institutions have been wrongly given authority. The church has become so enamored with these institutions that they are now placed on the same level of importance as is the knowledge of the Word of God itself.

Take seminary, for example. The need for pastors to be graduates of seminary has become so ingrained in the church that it's now the litmus test for who is "called" to lead God's sheep. These institutions dare to tell the church who is and isn't qualified to teach Scripture, and the church goes along with it. Nowadays, many churches won't place a man in the position of pastor unless he has a seminary degree. Why? Each apostle spent three years with the Word of God. That alone, coupled with the Holy Spirit, qualified them to teach us. If that was good enough for them, why does the church now believe it's not good enough for today's pastors?

Is the Word of God not enough to equip today's pastor for the role of shepherding? Or has pastoring become something it was never intended to be? Fueled by a society that places importance and status on those with "higher education," seminary has become the marker of qualification and prominence among pastors and teachers. Undeserved placement into the role of pastor or shepherd is based not on knowledge of the truth or a calling from God, but on a certificate given by men. The church, in turn, looks not to a man's life, but to a slip of paper. The tradition of formal education has come to outweigh proven character, wisdom, holy living, and rightly dividing the truth.

But traditions do that.

*"Jesus answered and said to them, 'Well did Isaiah prophesy of you **hypocrites**, as it is written:*
*'This people honors Me with their lips, **but their heart is far from Me.***
*And in vain they worship Me, **teaching as doctrines the commandments of men.'***
For laying aside the commandment of God, you hold the tradition of men."*
(Mark 7:6-8, NKJV)

The church "commands" that a man gets a degree before he can teach the Word. These are the "traditions of men."

*"Paul, an apostle, **sent not from men nor by man,** but by Jesus Christ and God the Father."*
(Galatians 1:1, NIV)

*"I did not receive it from any man, nor was I taught it; **rather, I received it by revelation from Jesus Christ."***
(Galatians 1:12, NIV)

And where can the revelation of Jesus Christ be found today? Am I saying that all pastors with seminary degrees are false teachers? No. Surely there are a few good pastors out there, and I believe God has truly called them to be pastors. But, if biblical history is any indicator, they are far from the majority. And, I would add, they didn't need seminary to get there.

Speaking of pastors, what is the job of a good pastor? Well, first, I can tell you what it's not. A pastor's job is not to spend time with God in our stead. That's *our* job. It's not a pastor's job to share with us the words and conclusions he learned at seminary from what other men have come to know about God through books other than the Bible. If God has called or sent you, then tell us what God Himself has told you.

It's not uncommon for men to be quoted during a sermon as much as—if not more than—the men of the Bible. It's as if quoting these men gives credibility to a view. Shameful.

A good pastor's job is to watch over his flock, to ensure heresy doesn't arise within his congregation—not to teach it himself. He's called to be a righteous example to his flock and the world, to build up the body of believers for the task of spreading the gospel, putting away sin, and living righteous lives. Through His Word, God gives these few pastors insights on how to practically live out their faith. But the pastor should be a *reminder* of what the Scriptures say, much more than an informer.

We, the sheep, should be in the Word of God *daily*! If that's the case, a pastor can't possibly share with us everything God wants us to know in just an hour a week, ten verses a week. Unlike the Christians of old, we have no excuse for not hearing from God directly. Thirty minutes of daily reading will get you through the entire Bible in about six months. But in a typical church service, only about one minute is spent actually reading Scripture—and that's weekly!

You and your local church shouldn't be in the same place in your readings unless you're doing no reading at all. And if that's the case, I question if your faith is real. The true follower of Christ is in the Word of God daily. We are all at different places in our walks with God. Do you think everyone at a church service is at the same point in their spiritual journey, or in their lives?

God reveals Himself and His truth over time, and we are called to do the work ourselves, "line upon line, precept upon precept." You don't need to be a theologian to understand what God is telling you. Don't be impressed that someone went to seminary. Most people going to seminary want to eventually pastor their own churches. Unfortunately, they believe they'll be better pastors for it. But "higher education," as far as God is concerned, comes from more time in His Word—not from attending college. You don't need a high IQ to understand God. He isn't impressed with our intelligence but with our hearts.

*"I praise you, Father, Lord of heaven and earth, because **you have hidden these things from the wise and learned**, and revealed them to little children."*
(Matthew 11:25, KJ3)

Do you see? The "learned" that you're so enamored with are actually at a disadvantage. As we see in the New Testament, which is our example, time with Christ (through Scripture and prayer), and obvious moral character ("seek first the righteousness of God, and all these things will be added to you"), is what qualifies a man to shepherd a flock. Qualification comes by spending time with Christ (i.e., in the Scriptures) and then being obedient to what He says—and we are all capable of that.

*"This is a faithful saying: If a man desires the position of a bishop, he desires a good work. A bishop then **must be blameless**, the husband of one wife, temperate, sober-minded, of good behavior, hospitable, able to teach; not given to wine, not violent, not greedy for money, but gentle, not quarrelsome, not covetous; one who rules his own house well, having his children in submission with all reverence (for if a man does not know how to rule his own house, how will he take care of the church of God?); not a novice, lest being puffed up with pride he fall into the same condemnation as the devil. Moreover, he must have a good testimony among those who are outside, lest he fall into reproach and the snare of the devil."*
(1 Timothy 3:1-7, NKJV)

Do you see anything in this passage about formal education? 1 Timothy 3:8-13 and Titus 1:5-9 also describe the type of men God wants leading or serving His church.

27

Nowhere do you find anything about school attendance or ministry and counseling classes.

When Solomon speaks in Ecclesiastes about the importance of seeking wisdom, knowledge, and understanding of God, he means *from God*! And where does any and all wisdom of God originate and reside but with Christ, His Holy Word?

*"Now when they saw the boldness of Peter and John, and perceived that **they were uneducated men**, they marveled. And they realized that **they had been with Jesus.**"*
(Acts 4:13, NKJV)

The apostles had no formal training after coming to faith in Christ. It would have surely ruined them. By including this verse, God wants us to see that formal education is not the key—time spent with Christ is.

I'm not a fan of the term "ordained minister." Who ordained them? A school system? Please. Each apostle spent three years with Christ. Yes, even Paul (Galatians 1:15-18). That alone qualified them to teach the church. Don't teach us what you've learned in school, a lecture hall, or from books. Teach us what you've learned from God's Word and nothing else. If that was good enough for the fathers of the faith, why does the church now believe that much more is needed for today's pastors?

Paul tells Timothy to keep up his study of Scripture because *that* is where salvation is found. Then he commends him to the work of evangelism. Nothing about schooling.

Is the Word of God too dated to keep up with modern times? Though they might not say it, many in the church act as though this is the case. God has given His true shepherds 66 books to study in order to teach His people. How many additional books do these institutions believe are necessary beyond God's collection to be considered "qualified" to pastor a church? It seems the church believes God needs man's help to produce a good teacher.

Do we think we know more now than God knew then? Does the modern seminary understand the modern man better and make the Word of God more palatable to today's churchgoer? Nowhere in Scripture do we see God advocating for seminaries or Bible colleges. How unnecessary! The Bible is our college campus; the Holy Spirit is our great Professor.

Contrary to popular belief, seminary is not a biblical mandate. Let me repeat that: seminary is not a biblical mandate. Yet too many in the church deem it so. Look at the state of the church in the West. Seminaries haven't curbed heresy, sin, or compromise in the church any better than before these Christian institutions existed. In fact, access to these "schools of higher learning" is greater today than ever before in history, yet the church is surely falling deeper into compromise. Pastors with degrees aren't doing their jobs. Today's Christians are no stronger in their faith than at any other time in church history, even though we have more pastors with seminary degrees than ever before—and God's people are just as rebellious and backslidden as ever. How ironic.

So, what's it all for? Just like secular schools of higher learning, Christian colleges and seminaries employ thousands of people, pay their professors top incomes, and take in billions of dollars. I believe Jesus would be appalled! God doesn't charge for His knowledge.

*"Come, all you who are thirsty, come to the waters; and **you who have no money**, come, buy and eat! Come, buy wine and milk **without money and without cost**. Listen, listen to **Me**, and eat what is good, and your soul will delight in the richest of fare."*
(Isaiah 55:1-2, NIV)

*"For we are not, **as so many,** peddling the Word of God; but as of sincerity, but as from God, we speak in the sight of God in Christ."*
(2 Corinthians 2:17-18, NKJV)

The salaries of both professors and far too many pastors make me angry. A pastor should make no more than the average income of his fellow church members. But how many of these men, who consider themselves "called" by God, would stand for that? I say, let's find out.

Seminary is a Christian tradition that has falsely come to be understood as a rite of passage from sheep to shepherd. But I ask, since the Holy Spirit combined with God's Holy Word is what Scripture teaches gives a believer spiritual understanding, why is a seminary necessary? You can't pay for the indwelling of the Holy Spirit, and without the Spirit, these seminary students will never understand the Scriptures correctly anyway. The Word of God says they can't. And in the case of the few who *are* Spirit-filled,

God has promised to give them understanding as they read the prophets and apostles! So, what need do they have of seminary?

"Now when Simon (not Simon Peter) *saw that the Spirit was given through the laying on of the apostles' hands, **he offered them money,** saying, 'Give this authority to me as well, so that everyone on whom I lay my hands may receive the Holy Spirit.' But Peter said to him, 'May your silver perish with you, **because you thought you could acquire the gift of God with money!** You have no part or share in this matter, for your heart is not right before God.'"*
(Acts 8:18-21, NKJV)

Yet, these seminary colleges say the opposite: "If you want biblical knowledge and understanding, pay up." It is my firm belief that if we closed every seminary school in the country, the knowledge of the Word of God and the morality of His people would not only *not* decrease in the church but would *increase* greatly within ten years. Why? Because Scripture itself—not the conclusions of other men—would once again need to be relied upon to give meaning and understanding to the children of God. But the business of "higher learning," as they call it, can't make money that way.

*"Now we have received not the spirit of the world, but the Spirit who is from God, so that we might understand the things freely given us **by God**. And we impart this in words **not taught by human wisdom but taught by the Spirit**, interpreting spiritual truths **to those who are spiritual**. The natural person does not accept the things of the Spirit of God, for they are folly to him,*

*and **he is not able to understand them because they are
spiritually discerned.***"
(1 Corinthians 2:12-14, NKJV)

The wisdom of God has never come from formal
education. I'm guessing that many, if not most, Jewish
priests over the last 3,000 years were formally educated
in "schools of God," and yet all of them are still wrong
in their theology, as evidenced by the fact that they have
not come to the conclusion that Jesus is the long-awaited
Messiah. All that schooling in Scripture hasn't done them
a bit of good, has it? Why do you think that would be? I
believe it's because they are not being taught by Scripture
but by men speaking in the place of Scripture.

And yes, of course, that happens in tens of thousands of
Christian churches every Sunday as well. In real time,
one or two minutes are spent reading the actual words
of God, and the other 45 minutes of "teaching" is the
pastor speaking for himself. And a college lecture hall is
no different.

Listen, it's good to have godly mentors, and of course, we
are to reserve our closest friendships for other Christians.
So, naturally, other people can influence our lives just by
the nature of those relationships. My concern, however,
is that the majority of those who consider themselves
shepherds are being influenced much more by other
people and popular thought than by the Word of God.
The beliefs they hold often stem from the conclusions of
others, who themselves were influenced by still others
before them. And so on it goes, little by little, the truth

and the message change ever so slightly, understood just a bit differently. But a slight change in the message creates other changes by necessity, and the domino effect takes over. This effect has had 2,000 years to run its course. Now, it's the norm. No one questions it because "it's just the way we do things. These are the conclusions we've all agreed to."

And the church will continue to lead itself further and further away from its foundation and into more and more compromise with the world and its wisdom. But since everyone is going in the same direction, nobody notices.

"They, measuring themselves by themselves, and comparing themselves among themselves, are not wise."
(2 Corinthians 10:12, NKJV)

To preserve God's original message, where are the pastors, the teachers, the theologians who have based their entire faith exclusively on their own reading of the Word of God? Is that a ridiculous thought? Am I being naive in asking that question? The Scriptures are the words of God—the only words of God that we have. Do they believe that? Do you? The Holy Spirit and the words of the prophets and apostles are where our understanding of God and our faith is to come from—by design! Not from any Bible commentary or famous theologian's interpretations preserved as if his book is an equal to the Scriptures, as if those books are spiritual works in their own right.

Do those in the church believe it is not possible, or even plausible, to understand the deep things of God by only

33

involving God? Is it irresponsible to hear from God in such a direct way? In fact, many preachers teach that very thing—not that we can't get through life on our own, but that we can't know God on our own, that we'll be lost without *them*. What egos! Is it naive to think the Bible, God's completed and infallible Word, is all I need? Sadly, I believe to the majority in the church, the answer to that question is "yes." And why would that be? Because I haven't been taught by men who've been trained in schools of higher learning? And people say I'm lost?

And why is it that so many teachers and theologians are influenced by so many other teachers and theologians? Could it be that they, too, are afraid of getting it wrong? Or maybe it's just easier to get the cliff notes. Is it embarrassing not to have an interpretation for every verse or passage? Christian, it is okay not to know the meaning of a verse or passage! But most don't see it that way. This is the problem with both sheep and shepherds. If a verse or passage isn't understood when being read, they've gotten into the terrible habit of looking up the meaning in some Bible commentary. And at that very moment, the answer becomes man's answer and not God's. They don't have the patience to wait for God to give them the answer in His own timing—most likely from somewhere else in Scripture ("precept upon precept"). But modern Christians, both sheep and shepherds, have no time for that. In this instant-gratification world of TikTok and two-day shipping, they demand answers now. But that's not how God has chosen to reveal Himself to His true followers.

*"**Whom** will He teach knowledge? And **whom** will He make to understand the message? Those just weaned from milk? Those just drawn from the breasts?* (The answer is: 'No, not them') *For precept must be upon precept, precept upon precept, line upon line, line upon line, here a little, there a little."*
(Isaiah 28:8-9, NKJV)

This is how God chooses to reveal Himself to each of us—not just to pastors so they can spoon-feed us, but to all His children. The canonization of His Holy Scripture has always been the plan. His shepherds were getting it wrong before Christ, and they've been getting it wrong after Christ. But the Scriptures never mislead.

It's why Jesus confronts the Jewish leaders and says, "If you truly knew and understood the Scriptures, you would know and understand Me" (words to that effect). God has given us the Bible as protection from modern shepherds. Let us hear the words of God, and let God give us understanding. That is what it means to trust in God! His words weren't available before in written form, at least not to the masses. But now they are. And since our history as God's people has always been to get it wrong—and often because of our own shepherds—now is the time for the sheep to break away from all these other voices and hear the Voice of God directly, as only the Scriptures can convey. This, His Word, is how He has chosen to implant His laws into our hearts and minds. We don't need these teachers anymore. Their time has passed. The Bible is the fulfillment of prophecy at last!

*"**I** will put My laws into their minds, and write them on their hearts. And **I** will be their God, and they shall be My people. **And they will not teach, each one his fellow citizen,** and each one his brother, saying, 'Know the Lord,' for they will all know Me, from the least to the greatest of them."*
(Jeremiah 31:33-34, NIV)

You, the church, assumed God was going to snap His fingers, and all the knowledge of God would simply be deposited into your brain, isn't that right? You assumed there would be no work on your part, didn't you? You never realized that the Bible, the canonization of Scripture, is the fulfillment of this prophecy. You just assumed this "writing on our hearts" by God was still some miraculous phenomenon that is set to take place in the future.

Christian people, the Messiah has come! The new covenant is here! And this—the Bible—is the promise prophesied about in Jeremiah! This is how God writes on your hearts. You've been waiting for something that has been available all along. And do you know why the sheep have never understood this? It's because, truth be told, they don't like the venue by which God has chosen to accomplish His promise. Nothing new here. And surely, all the influencers and teachers who make billions of dollars "teaching" you, and command so much respect, aren't too thrilled about this concept either. Nothing new there.

When God brought His children to the border of the promised land, the children just assumed God was going to snap His fingers and the land would be theirs. But that too was an erroneous assumption, wasn't it? And so, when He informed them that they would have a role to play in how He would administer His promise, that they would have to work for it, they wanted no part of it.

And now, here we are some three thousand years later, and God's people are still saying, "Lord, You do it all for us, and we will gladly, thankfully, take it. But if it's up to us, thank you, but no thank you. We'll just continue to make our neighbors and brothers our leaders and have them tell us what's going on, and what to think, and what we should and shouldn't believe about You."

Oh, you foolish people. God doesn't do it that way anymore. He has chosen to shepherd you Himself. And if you don't choose to do it His way, to accept His promise His way, then you are not going to enter the promised land.

David, in the Psalms we all love so much, gives only the Word of God—not any teachers—credit for his faith, his walk, his righteousness, and yes, his salvation. His commitment to the Scriptures available up to that point in time is what he himself credits with being filled with and displaying greater wisdom, knowledge, faith, and righteousness than any of the wisest men around in that time. And his words, like all of Scripture, were recorded for our learning, to be an example to us. "This is the way."

"You (God), through Your commandments, make me wiser than my enemies; for they (God's commandments) are ever with me."

37

(Psalm 119:98, NKJV)

*"I have more understanding **than all my teachers**, for **Your** testimonies are my meditation (not the testimonies of any man)."*
(Psalm 119:99, NKJV)

*"I understand more than the ancients, because I keep **Your** precepts."*
(Psalm 119:100, NKJV)

This "hearing God's testimonies," this "meditating on His precepts," does not happen via seminary, church attendance, or book reading—but only with time in the Word and adherence to it. If the church you are attending doesn't teach that the Word of God, and being in it daily (all of it), is far and away the believer's path to righteousness, understanding, and salvation, then run. Find one that does, and don't stop until you do. This will be a tough task indeed. Too many shepherds and sheep place far more importance on a man's Sunday attendance record than his time with God.

I am assuming that as far back as God's people have gathered together with other believers, instead of shepherds reading the words of God to the people (because it's the only way the sheep could hear His words), they most likely— like today—were taking a one-hour-long service to read a few passages from Scripture and then speaking from their own understanding for the rest of the hour. Is this "exalting Your Word above all Your Name"? No! They were, in effect, robbing God's people of God's words and exalting themselves and their own words, thus keeping the people from hearing from God directly and deciding for themselves the correct interpretation.

*"Therefore behold, I am against the prophets," says the Lord, **"who steal My words every one from his neighbor.** Behold, I am against the prophets," says the Lord, "who use **their** tongues and say, '**He** says."'*
(Jeremiah 23:30-31, NKJV)

The Isaiah passage in chapter 28, along with verses 10-22, reveals not only how, but why God reveals Himself and His path "here a little, there a little." He is weeding out His committed followers from those just looking for an easy way. To only those fighting vigorously to know Him, love Him, and yes, obey Him as He demands to be obeyed—He will reveal Himself, and only to them. He is very selective.

The true believer thirsts for His words! They love having their enlightenment grow "line upon line, precept upon precept." They look forward to it every day, just as God has said they would. But to the pretenders, reading Scripture will seem a mundane task indeed, and His precepts will be unacceptable, difficult, or even impossible to understand. Eventually, they will stop reading, and the result will be turning away from the words of God Himself, and instead following after myths and myth-tellers.

"For with stammering lips and another tongue He will speak to this people, to whom He said, 'This (Scripture) is the rest with which you may cause the weary to rest,' and, 'This is the

refreshing.' Yet they would not hear. But the word of the Lord was to them (pretenders), *'Precept upon precept, precept upon precept, line upon line, line upon line, here a little, there a little,' that they might go and fall backward, and be broken and snared and caught."*
(Isaiah 28:11-13, NKJV)

To His true followers, "line upon line, precept upon precept" is their food, their desire, their pleasure, and how God writes upon their hearts. But to the counterfeit Christian, "line upon line" is boring, confusing, and unfulfilling. The passage of time has not changed this spiritual truth. Instant answers are wrong answers because they don't penetrate into the soul of a man. When God Himself reveals something to you, it becomes yours to own. When the answer comes from another, even if it is doctrinally correct (count your blessings), it remains on the surface with no real power to change the heart. But when it comes from God, with understanding through the Spirit, it becomes yours to take ownership of. It becomes part of you.

I was once speaking with another believer, and one day she said, "Hey, Quinn, I was amazed this morning. I was reading the Bible, and now, for the first time, I understand what God is saying in this particular passage." To which I replied, "I've been telling you that for a year!" And she said, "I know. And I understood what you were saying, but now, all of a sudden, I get it!" Exactly! That's how it works! Not until God Himself gives you the understanding is it truly understood. She believed what I had been telling her, but I was the one giving her understanding, not the Holy Spirit. Now she believes it, "gets it," and most importantly, is more likely to live it out—because God told her, not a man.

"So the woman left her water jar and went away into town and said to the people, 'Come, see a man who told me all that I ever did. Can this be the Christ?' They went out of the town and were coming to Him... **Many Samaritans from that town believed in Him because of the woman's testimony,** *'He told me all that I ever did.' So when the Samaritans came to Him, they asked Him to stay with them, and He stayed there two days. And many more believed because of* **His word***. They said to the woman,* **'It is no longer because of what you said that we believe, for we have heard for ourselves,** *and we know that this is indeed the Savior of the world.'"*
(John 4:28-42, fragmented, ESV)

"The many" do not understand this concept, and they have come to trust others more than what God is showing them in their own time in Scripture. The theologians of the past have already agreed amongst themselves on what God has said and meant in His Word, and so the things of God are learned by those coming into the faith via third-party testimony. Naturally, the further we get from the original source of our faith, the greater the chance of getting it wrong. This happens when we listen to so many others speak of God, but they themselves are not God.

This is the trap! Jesus Christ *is* the Word of God! And He has become the stumbling stone, just as He said He would be. Listen, no matter how much you may like an

41

individual, you must refrain from relying on them to get fed. It is the words of Christ that feed the soul, not the words of man. He is the bread of life. He is the water we drink. He has a name, and His name is "The Word of God." And He alone is our one Great Shepherd, our One Voice.

ONE VOICE

"The words of the wise are like goads, their collected sayings like firmly embedded nails—given by One Shepherd. Be warned, my son, of anything in addition to them. Of the making of many books there is no end, and much study wearies the body." (Ecclesiastes 12:11-12, NIV)

I once came across a post on a social media feed attributed to a very popular Christian speaker and author, the late Timothy Keller. It speaks to a monumental problem in the Church of Christ today, and it is exactly what this Ecclesiastes warning addresses. The following quote, unfortunately, reflects popular thinking in mainstream Christian circles. This problem is systemic in the church. Here is Mr. Keller's quote:

"When you listen to and read one thinker, you become a clone... two thinkers, you become confused... ten thinkers, you'll begin developing your own voice... two or three hundred thinkers, you become wise and develop your own voice."

What a crock! Or is it? How can a man be so wrong and yet right at the same time? In his deception, he has unwittingly stumbled onto the truth and doesn't even see it. This is not what the Bible teaches about wisdom. This is what the wisdom of the world teaches. And it sounds wise, but it is folly.

"See to it that there is no one who takes you captive through philosophy and empty deception, **in accordance with human tradition, in accordance with the elementary principles of the world, rather than in accordance with Christ."** (Colossians 2:8, NASB)

"Take care that no one deceives himself. If anyone among you thinks that he is wise in this age, **he must become foolish, so that he may become wise. For the wisdom of this world is foolishness in the sight of God.** *For it is written: 'He is the one who catches the wise by their craftiness.'"* (1 Corinthians 3:18-19, NASB)

Mr. Keller was a professed Christian speaking to professed Christians! How ironic that this Christian seems to be against the idea of becoming a clone of someone else, and yet that is exactly what God has created us to become. Listen to one voice, and you become a clone? Exactly! Through the power of the Holy Spirit, by listening to the voice of our One Shepherd alone, we, the children of God, can become images of God. We are not put on the earth to listen to two or three hundred voices! Where is that idea taught in Scripture? We are not here to find our own voice. Show the biblical precept for that. We are not here to find our own identity. We are here to strive to be identified with Christ. We absolutely are here to seek and hear one voice!

The wisdom of God is available directly from God. To counsel believers to get "wisdom" by listening to 300 voices that are not God is heresy. This shepherd, this "thinker," believes the right way to come to an understanding about God is by hearing hundreds of different opinions or ideas and then each one deciding for themselves what makes sense? If this isn't New Age thought, I don't know what is. Do you see what's happening? The church—the sheep—are being taught by men who have been taught by men who have been taught by men, going back two thousand years! Christian, stop listening to the "experts," the "wise," the "learned," the "thinkers"! God has a collection of 40 authors He has personally selected, anointed, and brought together, and He put His collection of "voices" into one book just for you. There is enough theology, spiritual understanding, and direction in that one book for anyone's lifetime. It is inexhaustible, and it contains more knowledge of God and His will for us than all other theological and self-help books combined.

Yet fewer and fewer Christians know or believe in the full power it contains—that God counsels us through His words, and *His* words are the believer's connection to Him. *His* is the voice of transformation and the doorway to the Kingdom of Heaven. Salvation and wisdom are found in His Word and nowhere else.

"But as for you, continue in what you have learned and have become convinced of, because you know those from whom you learned it, and how from infancy you have known **the Holy Scriptures, which are able to make you wise for salvation** *through faith in Christ Jesus."* (2 Timothy 3:14-15)

Timothy learned from Paul. Timothy learned from the prophets. In this section of Paul's letter to Timothy, he is warning him of the many imposters in the church who deceive their followers and who themselves are deceived by others. You see, it's not that they are all purposefully lying, but that they are passing on lies that they believe—lies they themselves learned from others. It's why Scripture says they appear to be "angels of light"; because they often are very likable, amiable, well-spoken people. But they are wrong. And so, we protect ourselves when we listen to God alone.

Why has God chosen the written word over the spoken word as His form of communication with us? Why a book? Isn't it obvious? Man, His own creation, cannot be trusted. Not only have His people shown little ability to be faithful in their walk with Him, but they also have shown the inability to teach His commands and precepts accurately, much less obey them. One of the main reasons for this is that throughout our history, the children of God in charge of teaching and guiding the children of God are, in many cases, not "children of God" at all. Most of the prophets referred to in the Old Testament were false prophets—either self-proclaimed or ordained by some religious leader or party. They were not sent by God, but all professed to speak for God. The overwhelming majority of them were fakers or delusional. God spoke, and continues to speak, against these, the majority, throughout Scripture.

One obvious example comes from 1 Kings 22. Here, the king of Israel asks 400 "prophets of God" if he should go to war against Syria—a thing, by the way, he wants to do. All of them respond by claiming that God has told them he should go fight against Syria and that God will give him victory. The king of Judah, who was visiting the king of Israel, asks if there were any other prophets in Israel they could inquire of. There was one: the prophet Micaiah. Micaiah tells the two kings that all 400 prophets were filled with lying spirits and that listening to them would bring defeat and the king of Israel's death. And, of course, they trust the words of the majority over the words of the one. Shocking. Well, guess who loses the battle and dies in the process?

This is why the Lord has given us His written Word. It is the One Voice speaking out against the many. We don't have to worry about false prophets or bad shepherds leading us astray if we ignore them and instead have the written Word of God before us to refer to, learn from, and be guided by. Without it, we will quickly and easily be misled. This, I believe, is the condition the church is in now. It has been grossly misled. And that is the fault of both shepherd and sheep alike.

*"For the time is coming when people will not endure sound teaching, but having itching ears, **they will accumulate for***

themselves teachers to suit their own passions, and will turn away from listening to the truth and wander off into myths." (2 Timothy 4:3-4, ESV)

To "accumulate" is to acquire an increasing number of things. In this case, it is false teachers and bad doctrines. The church has had 2,000 years to accumulate an increasing number of "shepherds," until they, like throughout the history of God's people, far outnumber any true shepherds by an overwhelming majority. We have a shepherd, a teacher—the One true Teacher. This "become a thinker by listening to hundreds of thinkers" is, without a doubt, ungodly counsel and could not be further from the truth. Three hundred voices are 299 voices too many. God has determined that Scripture be the one source for our faith. It's the very reason the Bible is still here with us today. It is where Christ is found. To look for Him anywhere else is idolatry. These "men of faith" talk to each other, read each other, quote each other, and build on the writings of one another, while they have progressively moved further and further away from the one and only source of our faith: the Word of God. Every day, every week, every month, and every year, for the last 3500 years, these self-appointed shepherds die off. But the Word of God lives on!

All these voices of mere men have become the voice of the church. They've replaced Christ as the one voice in the church and will pay dearly for trying to usurp His authority. Because the sheep have chosen to listen to the voices of many false shepherds, they have wandered off into deceptions, lies, and ultimately a false gospel. God's people have always done this. And yet, even though God has given us so many examples, lessons, and warnings, the sheep still don't seem to learn or care. Instead, they say, as they have always said, "Speak to us smooth things, pleasant things." And our shepherds gladly oblige.

Because of the failure of our shepherds throughout time, Christ decided long ago that at His first coming, along with His new covenant, He Himself would take on the main task of shepherding His sheep. This He prophesied through Ezekiel. This is why we have the Bible today. It is the manifestation of Christ in written form; and it—His Word—is how the Son of God has chosen to shepherd us today. His Word is living! That means it holds the same truth for us today as it has for anyone in the past.

*"**Thus says the Lord God, Behold, I am against the shepherds**, and I will require My sheep at their hand **and put a stop to their feeding the sheep**. No longer shall the shepherds feed themselves. **I** will rescue My sheep from **their** mouths, that they (we sheep) may not be food for them (today's shepherds). For thus says the Lord God: Behold, I, I myself will search for My sheep and will seek them out. As a shepherd seeks out his flock when he is among his sheep that have been scattered, so will I seek out My sheep, and I will rescue them from all places where they have been scattered on a day of clouds and thick darkness. And I will bring them out from the peoples and gather them from the countries and will bring them into their own land. **And I will feed them… I Myself will be the shepherd of My sheep**, and **I Myself** will make them lie down, declares the Lord God. I will seek the lost, and **I** will bring back the strayed, and **I** will bind*

*up the injured, and **I** will strengthen the weak, and the fat and the strong I will destroy."* (Ezekiel 34:10-16, NKJV)

News flash: Jesus is no longer walking the earth. Not in the flesh. And His prophets and apostles—the only men on earth with God-given authority to speak for Him to us, whose words have the same authority as Christ Himself—are also no longer here in bodily form. So, the question that must be asked is, How do we hear from Jesus, the apostles, and the prophets today? How does Jesus, Peter ("feed my sheep"), and the other prophets and apostles feed us today? How is it possible for Jesus to be our One Shepherd, as He said He would be? The answer is, of course, the Bible! The Word of God and Christ are one and the same. But the church, to their shame, has turned to thousands of other voices from dozens of other sources to "hear from God," and our shepherds are no exception.

The Word of God is replete with accounts of God's shepherds shirking their responsibilities and/or leading His sheep away from the truth, and God taking them to task for it. I have listed only a few passages in this book that speak to this. But what of His sheep? What is our responsibility as His sheep? The answer: It is to make our Christian faith our own.

One church teaches this, another church teaches that. How many times have I heard, "Our church believes such and such"? That just makes me want to ask, "Yeah? Well, what do you believe?" Have you yourself poured through all of the Scriptures and come to the same conclusion?

50

Great! Or do you just accept it because it's what your denomination, your pastor, your parents, or the theologian you admire teaches? That's not great. That's lazy. In fact, that's dangerous! Lazy Christians make it easy for pastors, speakers, and authors to manipulate Scripture. You can't gain discernment without deep knowledge of the Word of God itself. And so many Christians don't have it. It's how heresy so easily gets a foothold. Make no mistake, we will all, individually, be held to account for our false beliefs. We won't be able to say, "Everyone around me was taught and believed the same things."

Who is supposed to lead you in your walk with Christ? Your church elders, some author, or Christ Himself? Well, Christ has just said in the last passage that He wants it to be Him! Christians, we are not led by the church, we *are* the church! We do not go to church to get saved. We get saved, and at that moment, we are the church, the body. Have we forgotten that? The "church," the "body," or the "bride" refers to Christians as a whole. We are His sheep, and He has come to lead us Himself.

*"And I have other sheep that are not of this fold. I must bring them also, and they will listen to **My** voice. So there will be one flock, **One Shepherd**… **My** sheep hear **My** voice, and I know them, and they follow **Me**."* (John 10:16, 27 NASB)

And who is "Me" today, but the Word of God? Obviously. Jesus is not here speaking audibly to the crowds these days, and the apostles are no longer writing Scripture. That was a very unique time in history. I repeat: The Bible was

51

always the plan. And it was a brilliant plan! It is the only way every generation can still hear Him. It is His voice!

"No more shall every man teach his neighbor, and every man his brother, saying, 'Know the Lord,' for they shall all know Me, from the least of them to the greatest, says the Lord." (Jeremiah 31:34 NKJV)

Praise God, those days are here! This is no longer speaking of days that will come later. The day has arrived! This is why this very passage is repeated in Hebrews. The apostle is telling us that the old covenant has passed and Christ has ushered in the new one—the new one with this promise as part of it.

I, Thomas Quinn Keller, am partaking of this gift, this grace from God, this promise. Are you? His law is in my heart. I am no longer in need of another man to teach me. How about you? For I sit at the feet of Jesus, the Word of God, every day. And so, every day, He Himself, personally, directly, is filling my mind and my spirit with His very words—no longer censored, corrupted, or edited by men first. And if you have been filled with the Holy Spirit of Christ and have a Bible within reach, you too can get in on it! No one is stopping you but yourself and your misplaced faith in men.

"I WILL PUT MY LAWS INTO THEIR MINDS, AND WRITE THEM ON THEIR HEARTS. AND I WILL BE THEIR GOD, AND THEY SHALL BE MY PEOPLE." (Jeremiah 31:33 NKJV)

This event that Christ is referring to, this implanting of His word into our hearts and minds, does not take place in an instant. Too many have made the erroneous assumption that, like the indwelling of the Holy Spirit, this will be a one-time and instantaneous event. And so, since it hasn't happened to them or anyone they know, they've come to believe that this is something that will occur in the future, perhaps when we get our new bodies. Because of this assumption, they don't worry about having "the Word in them" right now. Why would they if they believe they're going to get it all instantly at some future event? But they are mistaken. That would imply another covenant, one not discussed in Scripture. The word of God that is to be implanted in us by Christ the Word, is for living life in this world, in this age. So much, if not most, of God's concepts and precepts won't matter when sin and evil and temptation and false gods and prophets won't be a thing! The Word is for now!

This concept, this learning directly from God, has always been the only path to truth and understanding. They failed to see it back then, and most fail to see it today, even though God told them this was the case, and Christ still tells us it is true:

*"It is written in the prophets, 'And **they will be taught by God.**' Everyone who has heard and learned **from the Father** comes to Me."* (John 6:45 NIV)

*"Give us **today** our **daily** bread."* (Matthew 6:11 NIV)

Notice it doesn't say, "Give us today our Sunday bread."

*"As the living Father sent Me, and I live because of the Father, so whoever feeds on **Me** (how do we 'feed' on Christ?), he also will live because of Me. This is the bread that came down from heaven, not like the bread the fathers ate and died. Whoever feeds on **this bread** will live forever."* (John 6:57-58 NKJV)

Christ is our bread of life, not some theologian or pastor or church location. The bread itself was a representation of the Word of God, our "daily bread." That is what saves.

*"But He answered, 'It is written: Man shall not live by bread alone (material), but by every word that comes **from the mouth of God** (spiritual).'"* (Matthew 4:4 NIV)

Notice it does not read, "the mouth of men." This phenomenon, prophesied in Isaiah 54:13, that Jesus is referring to, this age of the new covenant, is not the next age, but this one. However, this implanting of His law doesn't take place all at once for all His sheep, at the same time in history. Instead, it has been building momentum over time as more Bibles have been made available. And with each of us, it happens gradually, as we partake of His bread.

It may seem slow to us, but it is in God's perfect timing. The apostles were finishing the completed words of Scripture. Then, there was the time between the last book and the canonization of the completed works. From that time, "The Bible" has been spreading, allowing more and more for Christ to take over the shepherding task from pastors, priests, and theologians—slowly but surely. Could it be that those teachers, pastors, and priests from Christ's time on, were a bridge from the apostles to the Bible? I believe so. God's glorious plan has come to fruition. Praise the Lord! "God with us," manifested in the written Word!

There isn't a specific moment in time that we can point to when this occurred, but alas, we are here. It's happening right under the church's nose. Seemingly suddenly, everyone has a Bible—the "Word of God"! Satan knows the prophecy has arrived, even if the "shepherds" within the church don't recognize or like it. Jesus has come to take His sheep away from the shepherds and shepherd us Himself, just as He said He would. Christ is our teacher now. He is our great Leader.

"But as for you, do not be called Rabbi ('teacher'); ***for only One is your Teacher***, *and you are all brothers and sisters. And do not call anyone on earth your father; for only One is your Father, He who is in heaven. And do not be called leaders; for only One is your Leader, that is, Christ."* (Matthew 23:8-10 NASB)

Remember when the religious leaders, seeing Jesus gain followers, had no interest in determining whether He was truly the Messiah? They wanted Him dead, fearing irrelevance and the collapse of their profitable enterprise. The heart of man is unchanged: "There is nothing new under the sun." This "One Voice" doctrine I espouse will never take hold because the powers that be will never allow it. Christianity has become an industry. The idea of the Bible taking over the teaching of believers will never be accepted by "the many." But this book isn't written for the many; it is for "the few," the remnant.

We, the few, haven't put our faith in the church or in men. We seek Christ, our One Shepherd. Him alone we will hear and follow.

"Truly, truly I say to you, the one who does not enter by the door into the fold of the sheep, but climbs up some other way, he is a thief and a robber. But the one who enters by the door is a shepherd of the sheep. To him the doorkeeper opens, and the sheep listen to **his** *voice,* **and he calls his own sheep by name and leads them out**... *He* (a paid shepherd) *flees because he is a hired hand and does not care about the sheep.* **I** *am the good shepherd, and I know My own, and* **My own** *know* **Me**.*"* (John 10:1-4, 12-14 NASB)

If you remember nothing else, remember this: In the beginning was the Word. The Word was with God and was God—from the spoken Word to the written Word, to the Word made flesh, and now the finished work—the very Word of God implanted in our hearts and minds. Jesus is the Word of God. The Word of God is Jesus. Through Scripture, Jesus shepherds us, the Spirit filled believers, today. The words of Scripture are how He feeds us, strengthens us, and implants His law in us. Without the Holy Spirit it's not getting in.

"For flesh and blood has not revealed this to you, but my Father who is in heaven." This is the manifestation of the Jeremiah 31 prophecy and others—the implanting of His laws. We who have answered His call are no longer in need of anyone to teach us this "living way." Yet most of mankind, including many who profess to be His children, do not wish to hear from God directly. They never have.

"Now when all the people saw the thunder and the flashes of lightning and the sound of the trumpet and the mountain smoking, the people were afraid and trembled, and they stood far off and said to Moses, 'You speak to us, and we will listen to you; but do not let God speak to us, lest we die.' Moses said to the people, 'Do not fear, for God has come to test you, that the fear of Him may be before you, that you may not sin.' The people stood far off, while Moses drew near to the thick darkness where God was." (Exodus 20:18-21 ESV)

Instead of the people hearing from God Himself, they preferred a middleman, and a middleman they got. And they died anyway. Until God's people—His church—take personal responsibility for each one's relationship with God, i.e., Jesus, i.e., the Word of God, personally, and stop trying to hear from God through a third party, His words and laws and concepts for spiritual living will never be implanted within the heart and mind. It can't be done through anyone but God. And this has always been the case. Those truly seeking after God know this to be true.

"I write these things to you about those who are trying to deceive you. But the anointing that you received from Him abides in you (the Holy Spirit), *and **you have no need that anyone should teach you**. But as **His anointing** teaches you about everything, and is true, and is no lie—just as it has taught you, abide in Him."* (1 John 2:26-27 ESV)

"Blessed are you, Simon Bar-Jonah, for flesh and blood has not revealed this to you (because it can't), *but My Father who is in heaven."* (Matthew 16:17 NKJV)

Even Peter, hearing the words of Christ directly, was never going to understand the words of God until the Holy Spirit got involved as well. The Holy Spirit and the Word of God are the way Christ manifests Himself today.

FUN BIBLE FACTS: (Information found on *OverviewBible.com*, taken from an article by Jeffrey Kranz)

The Bible was written over the course of 1,500 years—not one year, not ten years, but 1,500 years, from 1400 B.C. to about 100 A.D., by 40 individuals who lived in 10 different countries on three continents (Asia, Africa, Europe), in one of three languages. That may seem slow to us, but 1,500 years is only about a day and a half to God, right?

Worldwide, there are 80,000+ versions of the Bible, with full Bibles in 530+ languages and portions of the Bible in 2,900 languages. In whole or in part, the Bible is available to 98% of the world's population in a language they are fluent in. The Gideons distribute about one million Bibles, free of charge, every week!

There are 7.5 billion Bibles in the world. That's a Bible for every person. The Bible is not mentioned on any bestsellers list because all other book sales pale in comparison, year in and year out. It's not even close. One hundred million Bibles are printed every year!

The largest Bible factory in the world is a communist government-sanctioned NGO in Nanjing, China.

It is estimated that it takes 70 hours to read the Bible out loud. At the average reading speed, the Bible can be read in silence in 54 hours. (And yet, so many struggle to read the Bible in a year!) If you read the Bible out loud like I do, if you spend only one hour a day reading the words of your God, you can have the Bible read from beginning to end in 70 days. Heck, even if you only spend half an hour a day, you can still easily read through the Bible two and a half times a year! Most people don't read out loud. But the truth is, most Christians would rather someone else do their reading for them. "You go talk to God and tell us what He says." The Bible is God's plan. How committed are you to it?

I've held several beliefs over the years that I acquired just because they were popular conventions in the Christian church. Wrongly, I didn't question them. Now, I go to and trust in the Word of God, my "One Shepherd." It's what we are all called to do. I trust His Word is true and alive, and that He wants to personally teach me what He wills me to know through it. He wants me, first and foremost, to take His word for it. He speaks to each one of us the same message, but those messages are revealed in a particular order to each one of us individually. The order in which God chooses to reveal Himself and His way to me will most likely be different for anyone else. He is purposely building on precepts and concepts a little at a time as we are able and ready. I think in one manner;

you think in a different way. You need to work on these things first, and I need to work in other areas.

You give a child what he can handle. A teenager gets more and different things added that the child would not have been mature enough for. And yet, the teenager is far from knowing the concepts adults have come to know and need to know. We learn to add before we learn to divide. We learn to divide before we learn fractions, and so on. And so it is with the things of God. Only God truly knows what you are ready to know and what you are being held accountable to know, whether you actually decide to learn it or not. God considers where each one of us is as He reveals His concepts and precepts to us. And progressing in maturity is absolutely a requirement, so there is no standing still. Lifelong faith in God is a very serious business indeed. It is not to be taken lightly. God has prescribed just how we are to go about living out His faith. Remember, it is not ours—it's His, and it comes with an incredible amount of responsibility.

To "have faith in God" is to trust in His process. For this reason, I refuse to have a Bible commentary in my Bible. God put His Word together without any additional commentary. He says, "Do not add to it," and that, in part, surely is referring to all the extra commentary added to the Word of God by men. Shame on the church. Bible commentary is just someone else explaining to you what you just read, and, in effect, usurping the job of the Holy Spirit, who endeavors to use other verses and passages to interpret Scripture to the Spirit-filled believer. So, I ask, what's the point of God indwelling you with His Holy Spirit if you are just going to turn around and rely on man to tell you what God is saying? You might as well just read the commentary and leave God's Word out of it completely. These commentators do not trust that God can explain Himself to you. They believe He needs their help. Listen carefully. If God Himself cannot get you to understand what He wants you to understand, you're doomed. That is the charge of the Holy Spirit.

My Bibles have no commentary, nor any introductions to each book, or chapter titles if I can help it, so as not to bias me in any way. If God needed me to know additional historical background or any other pertinent information to come to the truth, He would have included it in the text itself.

Read Scripture, all of it, from beginning to end. And then start again. Study it. It/He is your salvation. Then, hold every person who professes to be teaching God's Word to account by testing everything they say against Scripture. That is a command from God.

*"Beloved, do not believe every spirit, but test the spirits, whether they are of God; because **many** false prophets have gone out into the world."* (1 John 4:1 NKJV)

I'm telling you, these false prophets have had 2,000 years to multiply.

"I know your works, your labor, your patience, and that you cannot bear those who are evil. And you have tested those who

*say they are apostles and are not, **and have found them liars.***"
(Revelation 2:2 NKJV)

Is He speaking of you? Are you testing these people who profess to speak for, or about, God? A pastor, if he is called at all, is called to watch over his flock and to give godly counsel to them. Your job is to know the Word so well that red flags go up any time anything contrary to Scripture is said. Your pastor is to correctly know the Word inside and out, as God Himself has taught him. But his words and counsel are to be supplemental to the Bible and your time in it. In fact, God's Word is pure food! Who needs supplements? It is your duty to God, and for your own self-preservation, to read and know His Word intimately. Otherwise, you run the very real risk of being led astray with the many. Blind allegiance to your church and church leaders is dangerous.

*"O My people! **Those who lead you cause you to err, and destroy the way of your paths.**"* (Isaiah 3:12 NKJV)

*"**For the leaders of this people cause them to err, and those who are led by them are destroyed.**"* (Isaiah 9:16 NKJV)

God is talking to us! What don't you get? Again, this is a pattern that has, and will, repeat itself until the end of the age. For most of us, when we came to faith in Christ, before we could build a foundation for our own faith from the source of that foundation, the Bible, we were told by others what it was we were to believe and what doctrines we were to hold to. We have been inundated with those doctrines ever since. So, instead of Scripture forming our beliefs, Scripture is interpreted in light of the conclusions we were already told to come to. Many have no doubt come to faith in a false gospel to begin with. We have been biased by the words and teachings of mere men from the start. The church is filled with millions of sheep living their lives believing they can't understand Scripture on their own. But the reason Scripture confuses them is that what the Word of God is plainly saying when they read it is not what they have grown up in the church believing. Or they are uncomfortable with what it clearly does teach. The Bible and the church's teachings become at odds with one another, and the reader gets confused and trusts man's conclusions over what God is telling them in Scripture. And they dare not question the shepherds and/or the majority.

So many Christians know what they believe, and no question they truly believe it, but they don't know why they believe it. That is to say, they believe because they have always believed it. They believe that the passages teach a certain thing because they have always been told that that is what they teach. It is what they were told to believe since they were baby Christians. But if we are going to know what we know to be God's truth, then we must, at some point in each of our walks, shut out all the bias we have come to know and come to the Word of God with new ears and fresh eyes and see what He alone says. It's how we keep our faith in check. If we are not willing to test our own faith by Scripture alone, then we, of all people, are the most foolish! As individuals, our faith must be our own, and not the faith of others.

I hope by now we can all agree that Jesus is the Word of God from the beginning. That the Word of God is a gift. But then Jesus also died for us so that those who came to true faith in God through Jesus would be forgiven. This is also a gift, a grace. Christ was then resurrected and returned to the Father. But, grace upon grace, He didn't leave us alone. He sent His Holy Spirit to indwell us and left His Holy Word to be completed by the apostles for us, which they did for the implanting of His law in us. All these things Christ did for us. Praise the Lord! But the one thing He did not do for us is live in our stead. This will be the topic of my next chapter.

SELF-FULFILLING PROPHECY

I was once corresponding with a woman who professed to be a follower of Christ. She made a point in our talks to make it clear that she was not perfect and that she hated "legalism." I asked her to expound on that. She wrote back to me with her answer, and when she was done, I wrote back a summation just to make sure she knew what she was saying and to ensure I had it correctly.

Here is my summation and her surprisingly honest response:

Me: Wow! Yes, you have made yourself loud and clear. I understand where you are coming from. You believe your true love for Christ is enough, that He accepts you for who you are today, that everything required of you He did for you. You are trusting in what He did and how He lived His life for your salvation. Did I get that right?

Her: BINGO!

This concept is prevalent in the modern church today. It is heretical, but not at all surprising.

"For the time is coming when people will not endure sound teaching, but having itching ears they will accumulate for themselves teachers to suit their own passions, and will turn away from listening to the truth and wander off into myths." (2 Timothy 4:3-4, ESV)

One very dangerous myth is this idea that the "commands" of God come with a wink. I came across this next quote a few times that someone or some group posted on Facebook. It was attributed to a popular theologian, but I couldn't confirm it when searching online, so I will not attach his name to it. It seemed unlikely to me anyway, but here is the quote:

"The whole point of our Lord's teaching was to show us that it was impossible. Had you ever thought of that? His teaching was just to show us that we could not do it."

Do what? Obey the teachings of Christ? The life God commands us to live—Jesus wants us to know we can't? Is this the conclusion we are supposed to come to when reading Scripture? If that was Jesus' point, why didn't He just say that? This quote attempts to climb inside the mind of God Himself and judge His thoughts and motivations. Obviously. For nowhere in the Bible does God actually say, "We can't do it," as whoever posted this quote surely believes. In fact, the Bible teaches the opposite. Those who believe this concept have not put their trust in the words of Christ (and by extension, His apostles). Because to not trust the Word of God to be telling us the true intentions of Christ's words is to not trust Christ, for He is the Word of God. I have no doubt that this quote, or at least this concept, comes from some pastor or theologian. But if this is indeed his take on Scripture, then he has made an incredibly large assumption, and then goes on to teach his assumption as biblical truth. I would not want to be anywhere near him when Christ comes back.

Now maybe I have this quote out of context. Maybe this is trying to say that Jesus is speaking of those of the world. And if that is the case, then yes, I would agree: for the natural man, it is impossible to live in obedience to the teachings of Christ (all Scripture). In this quote, it does read, "we could not" do it. And so, it is possible that he was speaking in the past tense. And if that is the case, then my apologies to whoever said this and those who understand him to be referring to our past lives before coming to Christ. My feeling, however, is that what he was getting at was not "could not," but rather "cannot," as in the present tense, for that is what the group who posted this quote was arguing for. So, I will proceed with that understanding. Surely there are many people who believe that to be the case, like the woman I spoke of to open the chapter. And they are the ones I will be trying to convince otherwise.

Let me make an assumption of my own. I assume that this theologian has come to this most heretical conclusion about the words of God because he sees that Scripture does indeed command that we, Christians, must be holy and obedient in this life in order to be granted entrance into the next one. This is what I assume he believes to be impossible. If he thought that the writings on their face taught that Christ did it all for us, and that faith, in and of itself, was our ticket to eternal salvation, he would have no need to come to the erroneous conclusion he has come to: that Spirit-filled believers are incapable of obeying God's teachings. So, the Scripture's teaching on its face must be obvious enough. They are to me. And so, the assumption must be that many of the Scripture's teachings must be of a facetious nature.

So, how could this man have come to this conclusion? I assume he has added another element into his decision-making process, other than the words of Scripture themselves, and it is this added element that has led him to believe that the overall inference of the Bible is that we aren't expected to live up to what it clearly commands of us. And that second added element, I assume, is…life experience.

Maybe this theologian is merely repeating what he had learned from theologians who came before him. Maybe he came to his conclusion on his own. But either way, surely he recognized that he himself was not able to walk in obedience to Christ, and this helped him come to accept this conclusion. And then he considered everyone he knew, and he didn't see them being obedient either. And they, too, knew of no one being obedient. This must be the case because if any of them were actually walking in obedience to Christ, none of them could say it can't be done, could they? And so, the conclusion all of these disobedient people have come to is that the Word of God must itself not be a command, as much as an ideal.

These men have placed their faith in experience over the Word of God. And that is idolatry. They have made life's experience the determination of spiritual truths, and then their conclusions, based on their temporal life experience, they preach as biblical concepts. It doesn't ever occur to them that if we need fleshly experience to prove a spiritual truth, then it's not faith; for experience is seen, and faith is not. And it is by faith we trust God's way is the way, not by experience.

Nowhere are we told to interpret Scripture with experience or to test the Scriptures by experience. We are told to interpret Scripture only with Scripture and to believe Scripture simply because it is the word of God. I personally have never heard a donkey speak, and I have never heard of anyone who has. Yet I believe a donkey can speak if God has a mind to cause it to happen. I have never personally felt or seen the earth stand still, but I believe it did, only because Scripture says it did. We need to consider nothing else but that when deciding if it is truth.

What is going on in the church? When it comes right down to it, here a Christian theologian is saying the Word of God doesn't mean what it seems to be saying. Or, to personalize it for you, God doesn't mean what He says.

So, let me get this straight: The natural man is born in sin and is incapable of living in obedience to God, correct? But the Spirit-filled man, who Scripture claims has been "freed from sin" and filled with the Holy Spirit of righteousness, is also incapable of living in obedience to God? What, then, is the point of our being converted? Why the indwelling of His righteous Spirit?

If God simply bestows on us eternal salvation the moment we believe in Him, then there really is no reason for anything that takes place after that moment, is there? And all epistles after the gospels are superfluous. If we cannot live truly obedient lives to God by the Spirit within, what power is there in the Spirit? Scripture teaches that the natural man cannot accept the Word of God; the "natural man" being anyone not filled with the Holy Spirit, whether he or she professes to be a Christian or not. This backward thinking would have us believe that the "natural Christian" (my term) wrongly tries to live in obedience to the Word of God, but the "spiritual Christian" knows it's impossible? I am confused. If experience is to be my guide in determining whether God's Word is to be taken literally or not, then my experience is telling me this next passage is on point and these teachers cannot be trusted.

"How can you say, 'We are wise, and the law of the Lord is with us?' Look, the false pen of the scribe (theologian) *certainly works falsehood. The wise men are ashamed, they are dismayed and taken. Behold, **they have rejected the word of the Lord; so what wisdom do they have?"*** (Jeremiah 8:8-9 NKJV)

They have rejected the Word of the Lord! Put "the wise men" in quotes. God's point is that these theologians, along with the people who follow them, consider themselves wise, but in actuality, they are fools. The sheep have placed their trust in false shepherds and not The Shepherd! The shepherds are telling the sheep, "Look, we know what the Word commands, but we're telling you it cannot be done, and God is cool with that. When He says, 'These things I'm commanding you today are not beyond you,' He says it with a wink." Doesn't that sound deceptive? Of course, it does. Any person is being deceptive, at best, if he says you can do something but knows you can't. But God would not deceive us. And so, the only other conclusion the believer can come to is, if God says we can, but we aren't, it's only because we won't. And why would we even try when our shepherds are telling us it can't be done anyway? Shame on them.

Let's look at a scene from Scripture that contradicts this false teaching that the commands of Christ cannot be lived out. It comes to us from Matthew's gospel. Some of the apostles are on a boat out on the sea, and they see Jesus approaching the boat. He is actually walking on the surface of the water!

"And Peter said to Him, 'Lord, if it is You, command me to come to You on the water.' And Jesus said, 'Come!' And going down from the boat, Peter walked on the water to go to Jesus." (Matthew 14:28-29 NKJV)

Did Peter defy the laws of nature and walk on water? You bet he did! And yet any human in his right mind would say, "That is impossible." And they would be right. Well, Christian, tell me, how did he do it? How did this man literally walk on water? And all God's people said,

"Faith." But how did he know he could do it? The answer is in the text:

"Command me to come out to You on the water."

Peter knew he could do it if Jesus commanded it. Can you or I walk on water? No! But Jesus hasn't commanded us to do that. He commanded Peter. And so, Peter could, and so, Peter did. Peter knew the biblical concept. It's why he asked Jesus to command him to do it. The concept taught is that if God commands it of us, whatever "it" is, it absolutely can be done. That was Peter's assurance! And God's commands are our assurance as well. Can you part the Red Sea? No, you can't. But God hasn't called you to that! That was specific to Moses. You can move a mountain if God commands it of you. But until then, it would be impossible. However, God has commanded each one of us, His children, throughout the entirety of Scripture, to turn from the practice of sinning and instead turn to a life of righteousness. And we can know it is possible to do it, through faith, because He has commanded it of us. Period. But you can't—or maybe it's more accurate to say, "won't"—if you doubt your ability. And that is the rest of the story, as Paul Harvey would say. Let's continue:

"And Peter answered Him, 'Lord, if it is You, command me to come to You on the water.' He said, 'Come.' So Peter got out of the boat and walked on the water and came to Jesus. But when he saw the wind, he was afraid, and beginning to sink, he cried out, 'Lord, save me.' Jesus immediately reached out His hand

and took hold of him, saying to him, 'O you of little faith, why did you doubt?'" (Matthew 14:28-31 ESV)

You see, when God commands anything of us, we cannot doubt that we have been given the power to do it, not just when the waters are calm, but during the storms as well. Doubters are weak and powerless to obey God.

"He who doubts is like a wave of the sea driven and tossed by the wind. For let not that man suppose that he will receive anything from the Lord." (James 1:6-7 NKJV)

It is statements like the "we cannot do it" quote that create doubt in the minds of many, leading the sheep astray. God's own words tell us that we can do it, that it is not too difficult, and that there were those who did it. Yet, we are told by these pastors and theologians that we cannot? Well, who are you going to believe?

"Woe to you, lawyers! Because you took the key of knowledge; you yourselves did not enter in, and hindered the ones who were entering." (Luke 11:52 NASB)

Do not listen to these shepherds! Our shepherds are killing determination! Your flesh wants to be able to continue in your sin, and you have found shepherds who will tell you that you can.

"Just make sure you feel bad about it."

"Oh, okay. No problem."

73

The church sings songs about "victory in Jesus" and "power in the Name," but so many of them are defeated and weak. How can they claim to have victory and power and at the same time consider themselves, and worse, be content with the idea, that they are "but wretched sinners"? How can both of these be true? The truth is, if after professing faith in Christ you are still such a sinner, you have no victory. The victory Christ gave His true followers is over sin! Scripture says that's the case, and yet our shepherds have thrown up their hands in defeat and say, "It can't be done." But they only say that because they haven't done it. And they can't personally know of anyone else that has done it, or they couldn't claim it can't be done. And that's pretty sad since "men of God" tend to hang out with "men of God." And so, shamefully, they believe their own experience over Christ, the Word of God.

The Word of God says Abel was righteous. Is God lying? This pastor and his ilk don't know of any righteous men in their own circles, but Enoch was righteous. That's two righteous men right there. What about David? God says he was a righteous man, "obedient in all the ways of God (that's what 'righteous' means), except in the case of Uriah." And then there is Job, of course.

"For there is no one like him on the earth, a blameless and righteous man, fearing God and turning away from evil." (Job 1:8 NASB)

Moses, Joshua, Caleb, and John the Baptist are all claimed by Scripture to be righteous men. Referring to Zacharias and Elizabeth, John's parents:

"And they were both righteous before God, walking in all the commandments and ordinances of the Lord blamelessly." (Luke 1:6 NKJV)

If the Word of God (i.e., Christ, i.e., God) says a man or a woman walked in righteousness, it must be taken as a fact, and as such, it cannot be argued otherwise. There are no other options! That these theologians and pastors know of no one walking in obedience to God is not a commentary on the accuracy or genuineness of the Word of God, but rather the sad and shameful state of most individuals in the church today. That must be the case because the Bible squelches all doubts about the ability to live in obedience to God by, one, telling us that it is indeed possible:

*"For this commandment that I command you today **is not too hard for you**, neither is it far off... But the word is very near you. It is in your mouth and in your heart, **so that you can do it**."* (Deut. 30:11-14, fragmented, ESV)

And two, by presenting people of the past who were obedient, thereby proving it is possible. Why would God tell us they were righteous if they were not? And how could they be righteous if true righteousness is not possible?

Now, let me give you a practical argument as to why your own experience may be that you might not know of any righteous people on the planet. Maybe there aren't any. "Had you ever thought of that?" Or, more likely, there are righteous, godly people on the planet living in obedience to God's Word today, but maybe they are so few and far between that you never hear of them. This planet does consist of other people outside of the sodomic West. Or maybe they are here. Maybe they live on your block. But since they have chosen to come out from the world, most Christians don't know them. You won't find them on Facebook or in your local bar, at clubs, or at the next Taylor Swift or John Mayer concerts. They don't participate in anti-abortion rallies, and they certainly do not protest the government or gather in political demonstrations. They live quiet lives, keeping to themselves, being at peace when at all possible, as Christ has called them to do. They rightly consider themselves aliens here and live as such.

God says Lot was a righteous man. But if in that time we were to spend a month in the entire city of Gomorrah, we would have found not one righteous person. Not one. Yet Lot was next door in Sodom the whole time. Going back further in time, had we walked the entire earth before the flood, we would have also concluded that living righteously was impossible. But yet again, there was Noah, living righteously before God. He was just the only one on the planet! But God says he was indeed righteous, even if he was one in a billion.

*"Then the Lord saw that the wickedness of mankind was great on the earth, and that every intent of the thoughts of their hearts was only evil continually... But Noah found favor in the eyes of the Lord... Noah was a righteous man, **blameless in his generation**. **Noah walked with God.**"* (Genesis 6:5-10, fragmented, NASB)

To say that living blamelessly in the eyes of God is impossible is defeatism at best, and worse, heresy, because it directly contradicts Scripture. The rarity of a thing doesn't make it not so. The extinction of a thing does not mean it never existed. Solomon declares that he could find only one righteous man in a thousand, and that was among God's people! Jesus pondered the idea that by the time He returned to earth, would He still find *anyone* who truly believed? And yet the church boasts billions of "believers?" Please. God created the earth and man, and things got so bad that He eventually killed off all but six people. That the other millions, or billions, of people who were killed were known to be evil did not prove one couldn't be righteous if he set his heart, mind, and soul to it. It just meant that the far and away greater majority chose not to.

Moses led a million people out of Egypt for the promised land. How many of them over the age of twenty, because of their obedience to God, actually saw the promised land? Two! But they did do it. The rest broke their covenant with God, so the promise was revoked, and they all died in the desert. God said, "These things I am commanding you to do are not too difficult for you." And Caleb and Joshua believed God at His word and determined in themselves to be obedient to God despite all the disobedience being lived out by the rest of God's people in their day. These two men stood on opposite sides of their own people, and for good reason, "bad company corrupts."

The Bible stories clearly reveal that the true disciples of God don't listen to the majority. They never have. They listen only to God. Today, God speaks to us through His written Word, not through men. But most Christians are interested in everything but that. Christ is the Word of God, and He is our great Shepherd. And He says He has defeated sin and death, and that if we turn from the world (so you have to turn from the world, a task most modern Christians refuse to do) and surrender to Him, and trust in His way (His way is difficult; it's just not *too* difficult), then He will forgive us all of the sins of our past and fill us with His own righteous Holy Spirit, thereby empowering us with victory over sin. We too can live righteous, obedient lives to God now and right up to, and into, "the promised land." It can be done, and we can do it! But we need three things after coming to faith in Christ to accomplish this eternal, and, evidently, very rare feat. They are, in no particular order, the Holy Spirit, the Word of God, and a daily determined striving after God and His will over our own flesh.

Obedience to God is not impossible for God's people; it's just improbable. There is a difference. But our shepherds don't believe it. And so, they tell everyone of God's people who will listen (and that is most) that obedience to God is not possible, and at best, it is a pleasant thought. And they have been saying it for centuries now. And now sheep and shepherds alike are convinced, and so they have given up even trying. And not only are they not trying, but they have been told that there is no need to try, for they have convinced themselves that the life Scripture calls us to live, Jesus has already lived in our stead. And so, not only do we not need to do it ourselves, but He doesn't expect us to. And then everyone says they know of no truly righteous people? Shocking. And if anyone dares to claim themselves to be righteous, they are thought of as out of their mind and/or conceited and prideful.

This "we can't do it" concept has become a self-fulfilling prophecy! But wait, this heretical, righteousness-killing doctrine gets worse; so that now, in the eyes of so many in the church, those few who teach we must live in obedience to God are called legalistic and are deemed to be part of a satanic doctrine called "works-based theology." The term "work," in the Christian church of all places, has become a four-letter word. If one like me insists that those of the church must practice works of righteousness, must give up sex, television, music, or even politics, in order to enter heaven, we are deemed, in the eyes of professed followers of Christ, to in some way be sinning because we are obviously not trusting Christ's "finished work" and are trying to "earn" salvation, even though Scripture clearly calls us to good deeds and to give up worldly living.

*"For we are God's handiwork, created in Christ Jesus **to do good works,** which God prepared in advance for us to do."* (Ephesians 2:10 NIV)

"Do not love the world or the things in the world (yes, Christian, this includes shows like Yellowstone and Game of Thrones and the like). *If anyone loves the world, the love of the Father is not in him* (His words, not mine). *For all that is in the world—the desires of the flesh and the desires of the eyes and the*

pride of life—is not from the Father but is from the world. And the world is passing away along with its desires, but whoever does the will of God abides forever." (Titus 3:8 ESV)

"What does it profit, my brethren, if someone says he has faith but does not have works (And the answer is, 'Nothing')*? Can faith save him?* (No)*... Thus, also faith by itself, if it does not have works, is dead* (James' words, not mine)*... You believe that there is one God. You do well. Even the demons believe— and tremble* (belief in Christ doesn't, in and of itself, set you apart from Satan)*! But do you want to know, O foolish man, that faith without works is dead* (what don't you understand here?)*? Was not Abraham our father justified by works when he offered Isaac his son on the altar?* (Answer—'Yes') *Do you see that faith was working together with his works, and by works faith was made perfect?* (Yes, I see that) ***And the Scripture was fulfilled** which says, 'Abraham believed God, and it was accounted to him for righteousness.'* *And he was called the friend of God. You see then that a man is justified by works, and not by faith alone.* (I believe James is telling the truth. Do you?)" (James 2:14-24 NKJV)

*"Let us be glad and rejoice and give Him glory, for the marriage of the Lamb has come, and His wife has made herself ready." And to her it was granted to be arrayed in fine linen, clean and bright, for the fine linen is the righteous acts **of the saints**."* (Revelation 19:7-8 NKJV)

If this "Christ did it in our stead" doctrine were true, then surely this passage from *Revelation* would say, "for the fine linen is the righteous acts of Christ." But, of course, it doesn't. Why? Because we will be judged on our own righteousness. Yes, the very righteousness given to us by Christ—that is, the righteousness we were to have "worked out" during the span of our lives after coming to faith in Christ. No, we as individuals are not credited with the life Christ lived. Why would we be judged by the life *He* lived? What proof of our faith would come from that? Christ Himself says His life was an example for us to mimic. His life was to be manifested through us. And Paul said the same thing about his own life! And what does Peter say?

*"Therefore, gird up the loins of your mind... **as obedient children**, not conforming yourselves to the **former lusts**, as in your ignorance; but as He who called you is holy, you also **be holy in all your conduct**, because it is written, 'Be holy, for I am holy.'"* (1 Peter 1:12-16, fragmented, NKJV)

*"To this **you** were called, because Christ suffered for us, leaving us an example so that **you should follow in His steps**: '**Who committed no sins, nor was deceit found in His mouth**'... so that we, **having died to sins**, might live **for righteousness**."* (1 Peter 2:21-24, fragmented, NIV)

"Having died to sins!" That means you gave them up when you came to Christ. At least you were supposed to. What don't you get? Throughout Scripture, God rails against "lip service faith." He insists on seeing it in our lives and takes no pleasure in our profession of faith in Him or songs of love for Him without our lives bearing that out in obedience to His laws and the rejection of our flesh. Otherwise, it is just lying, pure and simple. This false life in Christ is the very definition of "taking the Lord's name in vain."

*"And **by this** we know that we have come to know Him, **if we keep His commandments**. Whoever says, 'I know Him' but does not keep His commandments **is a liar, and the truth is not in him**. But whoever **keeps His word, in him** truly the love of God is perfected. **By this we may know that we are in Him**: whoever says he abides in Him **ought to walk in the same way in which He walked**."* (1 John 2:3-6 ESV)

He walked so that we could see how to—not so that we wouldn't have to!

(I have changed the word "gentiles" to "unbeliever" to make this next passage more relevant, since we do not call people "gentiles" today. You could also substitute "the disobedient" just as well.)

*"For the time that has **already passed** is sufficient for you to have carried out the desire of the unbeliever, having pursued a course of indecent behavior, lusts, drunkenness, carousing, drinking parties, and wanton idolatries. In all this, they are surprised that you do not run with them in the same excesses of debauchery, and they slander you; but they (the disobedient) will give an account to Him who is ready to judge the living and the dead."* (1 Peter 4:3-5 NASB)

*"**Do not** be unequally yoked with unbelievers. For what partnership has righteousness with lawlessness? Or what fellowship has light with darkness? What accord has Christ with Belial? Or what portion does a believer share with an unbeliever?...*

*Therefore, 'Come out from among them **and be separate,' says the Lord**. 'Do not touch what is unclean, **and then** I will receive you.'"* (2 Corinthians 6:14-17, fragmented, ESV)

*"Do you not know that **friendship with the world is enmity with God? Whoever,** therefore, **wants to be a friend of the world makes himself an enemy of God.**"* (James 4:4 NKJV)

These are not my words. They are God's, from the same Bible *you* profess to believe and trust in. Believer, the time for worldly living has passed, along with your worldly friendships. You must accept this. If you're still wanting to live that life, and you consider yourself a Christian, Christ says you are lying to yourself. And you are an enemy of God. His words. These passages are speaking to the righteous few and warning them to steer clear not just of those who profess no faith in our God, but just as importantly, those who profess to be "believers" but still do so much living for the world's pleasures. God, not me, says they aren't actually believers. These are those who are put off that we who are striving for righteousness don't participate in worldly living along with them. The ones who slander us are not as much those who claim no allegiance to God but, sadly, our own brothers and sisters in the church who have bought into the heresy that we can have our sin-filled cake and eat of the Tree of Life as well. And they think us prude, killjoys, and "legalistic" because we refuse to partake in their sin filled treats.

Take a look at verse 24 from chapter 13 in Luke:

*"**Strive** to enter through the narrow gate, for many, I say to you, will **seek** to enter and will not be able."* (NKJV)

Jesus says to strive to enter. To "strive" means to "make great efforts to achieve" or to "fight vigorously." Jesus Himself is telling us to make great efforts to enter the kingdom of heaven. Great efforts! So much for "Jesus did it all for us." So much for, "Say the sinner's prayer and you're in." Those who truly strive, who fight vigorously to enter, will be allowed to enter. But to simply seek without the effort is to condemn yourself. If one is truly seeking to know the way, God will reveal it. But knowing the way and striving to live the way once it is revealed to you are two different things. The modern church is saying it is good to know the way (that comes through seeking), but they believe it is a waste to strive for the way, even though Christ tells us to do it? That is anti-Christ!

Anyone who says it is impossible to live in obedience to the Word of God is not living in obedience to the Word of God. That is self-evident. And so, their own words condemn them. Then there are the few who heed the words of Jesus and have determined not to go down without a vigorous fight. We may or may not, in the eyes of God, end our lives being considered obedient servants like Noah and David and Job, but we are determined to give great effort to that end. And we will not be swayed by our own Christian brothers and sisters, ironically enough, who would deter us and think our striving is in vain at best, and at worst, living a false faith because of the audacity of our effort. They think it naive that we should try to "work out our salvation with fear and trembling." But we believe it is absolutely our duty to try and live the righteous path spelled out in the words of our God and King. It is a condition of the covenant we agreed to when we accepted His forgiveness for the worldly life we were living before our conversion. And we are happy to do it, for it is the least that we can do. He says we can do it, and the few, like Caleb and Joshua, take Him at His word.

*"So likewise, you, when you have done all those things which you are commanded, say, 'We are unprofitable servants. We have only done **what was our duty to do**.'"* (Luke 17:10 NKJV)

Christian, it must surely be our duty to obey His Word!

If you have convinced yourself that Jesus doesn't expect you to live righteously in this life in order to be allowed entrance into the next one—turning from the things of the world and obeying His words—then at the very least, live any life you desire. But stop telling those of us who desire to live obedient lives to and for the God we serve that it can't be done. Nowhere does Scripture teach that!

I have personally and painfully given up many pleasures of this world that I used to enjoy. And I am giving up more all the time. I have taken up many works of the Spirit that I used to dread—all because of what He has done for me and what He promises is still awaiting me if I live steadfastly, abiding in obedience to the end. AND because of the fear I have of what He says will happen if I don't. And because He commands me to do it, I believe it must be doable. Instead of telling me and those who believe as I believe that we are wasting our time, how about cheering us on? We need encouragement! The days are evil! Surely, it's not a sin to live doing as much for God as we can, to be reading and meditating on and discussing the things of God every day, and to be limiting our participation in the things of the world, since both of those precepts are commanded by God. Do you think God is really looking down on us, like some of you may be, and thinking, "Put that Bible down for a while and go watch *Game of Thrones* or *Fox News* instead. Why are you always talking about Me and My words and My ways when you have so many radio talk shows, online articles, TikTok, movies, books, sports, podcasts, and hobbies at your disposal? Instead of working at the hospital ward on your days off, go protest unbelievers somewhere, or picket the White House."

God's Word surely shows that the indicators of a true believer are reading His Word, meditating on His Word, and talking about His Word, and then, of course, living in obedience to it morning, noon, and night. Just read Psalm 119! Am I a heretic for heeding His words and trying to do that very thing? And yet many in the church would answer, "Yes" to that question. How backward professed "believers" have it. They are passionate about a false doctrine.

*"Brethren, my heart's desire and prayer to God for Israel is that they may be saved. For I bear them witness that they have a zeal for God, **but not according to knowledge**. For they, **being ignorant of God's righteousness,** and seeking to establish their*

own righteousness, **have not** *submitted to the righteousness of God."* (Romans 10:1-3 NKJV)

The righteousness of God is spelled out for us so we can't get it wrong! We are to read Scripture, behave in the manner He says to behave, and be who He says to be. By way of the Holy Spirit, God has implanted His very own righteousness inside the born-again believer, thereby debunking any idea that "it can't be done." Of course it can be done; we have the power of God in us! We are, of all people, without excuse. However, it's not enough to possess His righteousness; we must submit to it. If we don't, it is of no use to us or to God. Jesus said to fight vigorously to enter the kingdom of heaven, and after His resurrection, He armed us with the power to do so! It is the whole point of the indwelling! We couldn't do it in our own righteousness, but knowing that, He has graced us with His. And now we take ownership of it. What was His is now ours. That is the gift! Praise be to God! That is the truth that refuses to be acknowledged and believed by so many who profess to be children of God.

(2 Thessalonians 2:10-11) *"The coming of the lawless one is according to the working of Satan, with all power, signs, and lying wonders, and with all* **unrighteous deception** *among those who perish, because* **they did not receive the love of the truth, that they might be saved**. *And for this reason, God will send them strong delusion,* **that they should believe the lie**, *that they all may be condemned who did not believe the truth* **but had pleasure in unrighteousness."** (NKJV)

Do you see? Those who believe the lie still take pleasure in unrighteous things—all those unrighteous acts that you still allow yourself to see, to hear, to speak, and to participate in. How's your life looking these days?

There are two types of "Christians": those who believe "the truth" and those who believe "the lie" and so "continue to take pleasure in unrighteousness." Here God is contrasting one versus the other. To love the truth is to live it out just as much as it is to know it. That is what it means to "love the truth." In contrast, those "Christians" who are "delusional" (God's term, not mine) are the ones who have bought into the unrighteous deception. And what is the "unrighteous deception"? Well, it's the same as it has always been: *"Did God really say that if you disobey Him, you will surely die? You will not surely die."* It is this false teaching that disobedience to God's commands won't bring about death.

For the Christian, the darkness of this world has always been the forbidden fruit. And for most of God's own creation, they have sought out and found voices that whisper the same lie that has been whispered since Satan first walked the earth. This is still the most popular lie in the modern church today. It has been the same lie since day one. Adam and Eve believed the serpent's lie, and it eventually cost them their lives. How about you?

Be warned: The truth is the gospel of Jesus Christ. And the gospel of Jesus Christ is that the kingdom of God has come. As citizens of the kingdom of God, as children of God, we are to do what He says to do and be who He says to be. We are citizens of the Nation of Christ—the Kingdom of Christ. We are foreigners of this nation and this world. Kingdom living is living in righteousness. Hear this: It's not our forgiveness that sets us apart in the eyes of the world, but our righteousness. Forgiveness, like the Holy Spirit, can't be seen—only our righteousness can! Those who have been allowed into the Kingdom because of the shed blood of Christ and yet still make it a practice of pleasuring themselves with the sins and excesses of the world will be condemned. Do not listen to anyone who says, "You can't do it." The Word of God clearly teaches you can, and you must.

One of the biggest lies in the church is this well-known saying, "I'm just a sinner saved by grace." For the Christian to admit he/she is a sinner is to admit he/she is not truly a believer at all. Scripture is clear that those who are in the practice of sinning (i.e., a "sinner") will not enter the Kingdom of Heaven. So how can both be true? How can one consider themselves a sinner and yet still think they will be admitted entrance into heaven? This will be the focus of my next chapter. It is my attempt to shine biblical light on the idea of instant assured salvation with little to no consideration of the proofs of kingdom citizenship.

THE SINNER'S PRAYER

(Jesus, explaining the latter part of the parable) *"Hear then the parable of the Sower: What was sown on rocky ground, this is the one who hears the word and immediately receives it with joy, yet he has no root in himself, but endures for a while, and when tribulation or persecution arises on account of the word, immediately he falls away. As for what was sown among thorns, this is the one who hears the word, but the cares of the world and the deceitfulness of riches choke the word, and it proves unfruitful. As for what was sown on good soil, this is the one who hears the word and understands it. He indeed bears fruit and yields, in one case a hundredfold, in another sixty, and in another thirty."* (Matthew 13:18-23, fragmented, ESV)

One of the tragedies of placing your eternal security in the conclusions of men is that you begin to build a foundation based on their conclusions, through which all Scripture suddenly must flow. Instead of running the words of a man through the filter of Scripture to see if it is true, the believer becomes conditioned to run Scripture through the filter of what a man, or a consensus of men, teaches as doctrine. What then happens, and I believe happens more often than not, is that all passages containing precepts or concepts not taught within the church's teachings are labeled as "hard to understand" or "commonly misunderstood." When a church is conditioned to accept whatever is coming from the pulpit, a culture is formed that becomes truth within itself. Most don't even consider that the church's teachings could be in error.

With this in mind, one of the deadliest doctrines of the church that has popped up in the last century is a little (but not so little) thing called **the sinner's prayer**.

Here comes a chapter that is going to rub many believers the wrong way—not that I haven't already. Let me say first, I do not want anyone thinking I am aligning them personally with Satan. I absolutely am not. I am saying, however, that all bad doctrine is Satan's doctrine. He wants us to understand the gospel, the message, and the commandments wrongly. Agreed? ("You shall not surely die.") His goal is to replace good doctrine and practices with bad, or at best, useless ones. It doesn't do any good to attempt that with the world. What good would it do? The world is already going to hell. In that respect, things are going well—why mess up a good thing? Satan's desire is to destroy the church. The church is the enemy, not the world. So how could he go about doing that?

Let's pick a doctrine that many Christians seem to agree is biblical: the doctrine of "once saved, always saved." If this doctrine is false, with so many Christians believing it to be true, it would be one of the greatest lies Satan has perpetrated on God's church. Since our flesh greatly prefers the easier path to the difficult, Satan, all too aware, uses this preference of ours to seduce the church away from truth and into a lie. Coming as an angel of light, he dresses his lies up in flowery terms. He's the master of manipulation and has many accomplices who also dress in light. They are most often, but not always, attractive people—easy on the eyes, amiable, smart, warm, funny, popular people. People who are easy to believe and follow. They are well-liked and are, very often, popular Christians. And they all have one thing in common: they are liars. Whether intentionally or unintentionally, they spread lies.

Instead of focusing on the importance of daily obedience and spiritual growth in the individual, the doctrine of "once saved, always saved" changes the primary focus from holiness and godliness to resting in the comfort of your assured eternal salvation. "Always remember you are saved, no matter what. As long as you 'believe' you can never lose your salvation. Therefore, go out and make other converts." And these new converts become even worse sinners than they were before coming to Christ because to possess the knowledge of good and evil and still sin is a much greater crime than all sins of ignorance.

Modern Christianity has merely become a numbers game. We need to get people "saved," so what is the quickest and easiest way to do that? Enter "the sinner's prayer."

I envision it going this way: Satan, disguised as "an angel of light," sneaks into the church and, under the guise of God's grace and mercy—coupled with all the other wonderful attributes that God indeed possesses—is allowed to start twisting existing Scripture. He places an ounce of truth in a pound of lie. People are then taught that once "saved," even if we should continue to live as sinners, because of His grace and mercy, He will never take our salvation from us. That wasn't the lesson of Israel, but whatever. Well yes, that does sound wonderful! And easy! And it's the "easy" that makes it easy for people to buy into it.

The minute we come to faith in Christ, we are so often immediately told that we have just changed over from death to life, that we have been born into the family of God, never to fear death again. If you were looking for an easy religion, brother, you have found it! This, however, is wrapped in a lie designed to destroy the Christian.

Let me illustrate it for you:

A young woman is walking around in a life of sin leading to death when a friend asks her to come hear this charming speaker giving a talk at a local high school football stadium. Even though she goes only because she's asked, the speaker's words actually make sense to her, and before she knows it, she's walking onto the field with 50 other people and is led in a prayer to ask Jesus to forgive her of all her sins, to come into her heart, and to be the lord of her life (not that she really knows what "lord" means).

There, she did it. In the span of an hour-long talk and a two-minute prayer, she is said to have gone from the walking dead to immortality. Congratulations! As soon as she finishes her prayer, Satan starts in with his lie (spoken through the same evangelist who had led her in the prayer moments earlier): "If you truly meant what you said, then by the grace of God, you have been forgiven and have been given eternal salvation, and there is nothing you can ever do to lose it from this moment on." Isn't that the script? The message? She has only been a Christian for 30 seconds, and Satan, with help from well-meaning but doctrinally wrong Christians, has already planted the seed of rebellion. He is relentless! She had better dive into the Scriptures and stay there, because from here on out, she has become priority number one to Satan. You see, he didn't care what she did as a sinner, but now that she is a child of God, she has changed teams and has instantly become the enemy. He will not stop until the day she goes to see the Lord or the day she turns back to the world—whichever comes first.

Fast forward: Three or four years have passed. She seemed to be doing well in her walk with Christ. However, she has just moved to a new state and/or started a new job. An opportunity, which she should probably not take advantage of, comes up. Maybe it's going out for drinks to a new club with her new workmates—maybe it's something else. The point is, she knows it's probably not where God would have her go or with the people He would have her go with, but still, something or someone in the back of her mind says, "Oh, it's not that big a thing, girl. You should go, get out, have some fun. You'll be careful not to let it go too far." She decides to go and actually has a pretty good time. The people, although not Christians, are fun—especially Bob. He's so funny. And cute too! You see where this is all going? That's how it starts. The further she goes with it, the more she reminds herself of the words spoken on the day she "placed her faith" in Christ and many times since: "There is nothing you can ever do to lose your salvation."

Fast forward another two years. That little voice in the back of her head has now given her permission over and over to go deeper and deeper into her sin life and further and further away from God. Bob is her boyfriend now. He's the best! So funny. So smart. Very intellectual. As it turns out, he's no believer at all—not in God anyway. He is, however, a firm believer that religion is just an escape drug for people who can't handle science. Completely buying into him and his life, she no longer talks with her old friends and rarely gives God a thought, except to remind herself, "Once saved, always saved," which strangely comforts her. Another win for Satan. He'll keep his eye on her every now and then, but he's got bigger fish to fry. She is no longer a danger to furthering God's kingdom now that she is back in his world.

(I replaced "she" for "he") *"For if, after she has escaped the pollutions of the world through the knowledge of the Lord and Savior Jesus Christ, she is again entangled in them and overcome, the latter end will be worse for her than the beginning. For it would have been better for her not to have known the way of righteousness than having known it, to turn from the holy commandment given to her. But it has happened to her according to the true proverb: 'A dog returns to her own vomit,' and 'a pig, having washed, to wallowing in the mud.'"* (2 Peter 2:20 NKJV)

This illustration of the young lady is exactly what this passage from 2 Peter is warning us to stay clear of. **Conversion salvation** (drawing you out from the sins of this world and purifying your soul of past sins) is no guarantee of **eternal salvation** (saving you from God's eternal damnation and into the kingdom of heaven). This story illustrates an all-too-common occurrence in real life; people come to the faith with the best of intentions but then fall away when the events of life occur. And no, the story need not be as dramatic as denouncing the faith. Still living as a sinner while professing Christ will do just fine. Since we don't all handle what life can throw at us the same, imagine the relief it brings to be told that we are assured the reward no matter how we have lived.

If someone is worried about what happens to them when they die and we tell them we have the answer to that question, and then go on to tell them that they can have heaven for eternity if they say and believe, and earnestly mean, a two-minute prayer, then we are telling them, in effect, that nothing is required of them from that moment on. Think about it: if during this life our salvation could ever be locked up, then at that very moment we become forever free to ignore Christ's commands. We are, in a sense, saying to the new believer and all believers, "Welcome to your life in Christ. It is finished!" Their new faith is defeated before it ever gets out of the box.

They may have been made clean, but the perfecting process of being conformed into the image of Christ by the Holy Spirit through a steady diet of God's word, righteous deeds, and the putting away of sin so often never even gets started. I know many professed Christians in this category.

Nowhere in the New Testament is anyone led in a prayer to come to Christ, nor is this type of prayer taught or commanded. The church came up with this prayer idea relatively recently, and it quickly became the litmus test for determining if someone is a believer or not. It isn't! Yet, pastors will routinely take people through this "sinner's prayer" and tell them, if they meant it, then Jesus says they have been forgiven of their sins and have just received the free gift of eternal salvation. It's as if Jesus Himself gave us the "sinner's prayer" just like He gave us the "Lord's Prayer." Well, He didn't. It's just a church tradition masquerading as doctrine.

I have been in so many services where the pastor so obviously manipulated people to come up front and repeat a prayer to ask Jesus into their hearts. I literally get a sick feeling as soon as this show starts. At first, while still standing at their seats, they are merely told to raise their hands while everyone's eyes are closed so that the pastor can pray for them. They are made to believe that is going to be all that is asked of them. But step by step, the pastor continues his skillful manipulation until that person has been pressured to come all the way up front and be paraded in front of the church, led in a prayer while everyone's watching to see if they repeat it, and then led away into a room where they will be told of all the wonderful programs and "new believer" classes they should attend at that particular church. That is not where he or she thought it was all going when raising his or her hand. They were tricked, plain and simple. But I guess it's okay if it's for Jesus?

So many people are presented with a counterfeit gospel to begin with, and that is the gospel they place their faith in. And the church applauds and puts up another tally on the board for God, but these people were never introduced to the true gospel. They were instead introduced to a fantasy. They were never told, while they were being presented the gospel, to consider long and hard about what they were about to commit to: that to come to Christ is to give up their lives as they know them, die to their own dreams and desires, and fully embrace life in the kingdom of God, away from the lustful pleasures that are so enjoyed by everyone around them in the world. That repentance must come first isn't explained, defined, or, so often, even mentioned before "leading" someone to Christ. So, how can they know what they are being called to? Because you didn't explain what they were getting into, you have damned many of them worse than had they never come to Christ in the first place! And that is on you, pastor or evangelist.

"Whoever does not bear his own cross and come after me cannot be my disciple (we could stop right there because He's just lost most Christians). *For which of you, desiring to build a*

*tower, does not first sit down **and count the cost, whether he has enough to complete it?** Otherwise, **when he has laid a foundation** and is **not** able to finish, all who see it begin to mock him, saying, 'This man **began** to build (verb) **and was not able to finish**.'"* (Luke 14:27-30 NKJV)

*"If anyone comes to Me and **does not** hate his father and mother, wife and children, brothers and sisters, yes, and his own life also, **he cannot be My disciple."*** (Luke 14:26 NKJV)

*"He who loves mother or father or son or daughter more than Me **is not worthy of Me**."* (Matthew 10:37 ESV)

*"Anyone who wishes to come after me **must** deny himself, **and let him take up his cross**, and let him **follow** me."* (Matthew 16:24 KJ3)

"For whoever desires to save his life (wants to continue to live as he wants to live) *will lose it* (will go to hell eternally), *but whoever loses his life* (freely gives up his desires and goals and plans, and former ways of sinning, and instead lives by the teachings of God) *for my sake and the gospel's will save it* (will live eternally in heaven)." (Mark 8:35 NKJV)

Why aren't these passages read out loud before asking people to come up front and profess faith in Christ? Because we all know very few are interested in the type of surrender Christ has called His followers to. The true followers of Christ in any local body of believers need only about ten percent of the real estate at most churches. In truth, a big enough family room in a person's home will fit them all. The basic gospel is our foundation, absolutely. But that foundation is for nothing if we don't build our house on top of it! A washed spirit (our initial forgiveness) is certainly the *only* way to get the foundation we must have in order to build our house. But that house *must* be built! The Christian who comes to faith without considering all that they will have to give up and take on will most likely fall away, assuming they ever actually step onto that difficult and narrow path in the first place. Oh, he or she may profess faith for the rest of their lives, but their words, in and of themselves, are not what determines a true disciple. This is absolutely what Jesus is getting at in these passages. No, eternal salvation in this temporary-life-stage is not free. It comes at a great cost! Nobody said it was free. Jesus gave the entirety of His life for you. In return, you must give whatever time you have left on this earth to Him. Still interested?

A vital question that needs to be asked when talking about a "sinner's prayer" is: Does eternal salvation happen in an instant, or throughout the course of our life? If it happened to the girl in my made-up story in an instant, through an earnestly meant prayer, are we to believe that Christ was obligated to indwell her with His Spirit as soon as she believed the gospel? What happens if she, on her way home, is hit by a train and dies? Will she be, like the "thief on the cross," bound for paradise? If your answer is yes, then let's change the ending of the story and say she doesn't get hit by the train and makes it home safely. Upon arriving home, she opens her brand-new Bible and starts to see what God is asking of her as a follower of Christ. What if, after six months of reading the Word and having "counted the cost," as Christ has counseled her to do, she decides, "No dice. The deal is off." She quite enjoys her fleshly life and has no intentions of giving it up, thank you very much. What if she puts down that Bible and never picks it up again? Is she still considered eternally saved? Is her salvation still secure? If you say, "Well, in that case, she was never saved to begin with," then you're saying she also wasn't saved before she had been killed by the train just 6 months earlier. Correct? You can't have it both ways. Eternal salvation must require more than "really meaning" a two-minute prayer. Only the time we've been allotted over our entire life can decide. And, by the way, that could just as well have gone for the thief on the cross. Jesus absolutely knew that man was not coming down off of that cross alive, and that is how He knew for sure that man's faith was going with him to the grave.

Pastors and evangelists desire to lay out a quick and easy path of faith that can be completed in one morning service. Short and easy is never mentioned in relation to faith anywhere in Scripture. In fact, the quickest way to kill any believer's faith is to tell them they've "arrived." Surely, it's why Satan loves and propagates the sinner's prayer. If Philippians weren't in the Bible, and I were to say the following words of Paul today in most churches, I would surely be labeled a heretic.

Me, standing behind the pulpit as a guest speaker during your church service (pretend you are hearing these words for the first time):

"*For His sake I have suffered the loss of all things and count them as rubbish, in order that I may gain Christ and be found in Him,* (Hey, Quinn, you didn't have to do all that. Just a simple earnest prayer would have sufficed.) *not having a righteousness of my own that comes from the law, but that which comes through faith in Christ, the righteousness from God that depends on faith—that I may know Him and the power of His resurrection, and may share His sufferings, becoming like Him in His death,* **so that by any means possible I may attain the resurrection from the dead.** (Oh, don't worry about that, Quinn. Don't you know it's a guarantee?) **Not that I have already obtained this** (Wait, what was that?) *or am already perfect,* **but I press on to make it my own,** *because Christ Jesus has made me His own.* **Brothers, I do not consider that I have made it my own.** (Quinn, if you believe in Christ, you have—you have!) *But one thing I do: forgetting what lies behind* **and straining forward** *to what lies ahead,* **I press on toward the goal** *for the prize of the upward call of God in Christ Jesus.* (Quinn, you have the prize. What are you straining so hard for?) **Let those of us who are mature think this way,** *and if in anything you think otherwise, God will reveal that also to you. Only let us hold true to what we have attained* (so far)." (This guy has it all wrong. Can someone get him off the stage? He's making this seem much more difficult than it is!) (Philippians 3:8-16 ESV)

We must rethink this doctrine of "once saved, always saved." In the parable of The Sower and the Seed, the first person never came to true faith. The last three "soils," however, gladly accepted the seed (the Word of God). The last three believed, but only one produced fruit; the implanted seed died out in the other two. While some evidence of change was likely there at the beginning with these two, outside influences and fleshly desires came and destroyed the life growing inside. The lesson here is "endurance." Those who do not put away the world, but allow it to choke out the seed, the life of Christ, are by Christ's definition not enduring. And it's only in the enduring that eternal life will be waiting for us. Yet, if the people represented by these two seeds were to have come to faith in so many of today's churches, they would have been told that their eternal salvation was theirs, eternally locked-up from that moment on, contrary to what Christ teaches in the parable.

*"The one who received the seed that fell on rocky places is the man who **hears the word** and at once receives it with joy. But since he has no root, he lasts only for a short time. **When trouble or persecution comes because of the word, he quickly falls away.**"* (So did he ever have salvation?) *"The one who received the seed that fell among the thorns is the man who **hears the word*** (acceptance of it inferred), *but the worries of this life and the deceitfulness of wealth choke it, making it unfruitful."* (So did he ever have salvation?) *"But the seed that fell on good soil is the man **who hears the word and understands it**. He produces a crop, yielding a hundred, sixty, or thirty times what was sown."* (Matthew 13:20-23 NASB)

It is only in enduring faith—and all that stands for—that salvation is assured! This is how time plays its role. In the parable of the seeds, Satan managed to keep the Word of God from ever being planted in the first person. The second two, however, started to grow in their faith and so took longer to fall away, but fall away they did. Why? Because Satan is relentless. He won't stop. It's why we are warned never to let our guard down, to persevere, to endure. "Enduring" does not mean "stay alive until we die"; everyone in the world does that! We are to endure all of life's temptations, not all of life's sins. You must see the difference! Temptation will be coming at us our entire life with the very purpose of leading us into sin. Why is that? Because the practice of sin leads to death. If, as Christians, we are now immune from what God calls "the law of sin and death," why would Satan bother coming at us? Why would he want us to keep sinning if he knows it will have no effect on our eternity? The answer is because he knows no such thing! This is why believers are warned to be aware of the prowling lion; the devil knows it is possible for us to be taken from life to death, from being washed clean to wallowing in the mud again. And of course this is possible, or Peter wouldn't have warned us of it. And speaking of Satan—make no mistake, Satan was not an unforeseen adversary. He has a role to play, by design.

TANGENT ALERT! So, what is Satan's role? I believe Satan is a tool of God. He is not one of two gods, one being evil and one being righteous. Only God is God, and Satan was created by God just like you and I were. He is not equal in any way to the Father, the Son, or the Holy Spirit. He has no power but what God gives him at any time. Satan is not free to do what he wants when he wants. When he comes against a believer, it is always with God's permission. His actions do not happen without the foreknowledge of God and are always used to accomplish God's purpose. God is continually sifting the wheat from the chaff and testing us so that the true condition of our hearts and the earnestness of our convictions are revealed. Satan plays a big role in that.

In the gospel of Luke, Satan asks for permission to sift Peter. God does not deny his request, but instead, Jesus prays for Peter, knowing the test that is coming. This passage (Luke 22:31-32) is not only about the failure of Peter during this test, but it also shows us that Satan does not act without permission. Remember the story of the man possessed by the legion of demons? The demons possessing the man in chains asked permission to go into a herd of pigs. They knew who their authority was and that they needed permission from Him before they could move. They could not act on their own. In Job, chapters one and two, we see the same thing happen. Twice, Satan asks for permission to test Job—to inflict him with severe suffering. God gives him permission to kill Job's family, wipe out all his wealth, and cause prolonged, agonizing pain upon him. God granted it! And this against one of God's chosen, whom He calls the most righteous man on earth. And what about Jesus? As soon as Jesus was filled with the Holy Spirit, the Spirit Himself led Christ right to Satan for the very purpose of allowing Satan to tempt Him day in and day out! And this was no perfunctory test. It mattered—for the salvation of every believer, and even for Jesus Himself.

Why would God allow such things to happen to those He loves? One reason: He is creating men and women into a new form of super-being. Jesus Himself had to go through the same testing, sufferings, and temptations as we do in order that He too could become part of this special creation called the Children of God. His life was not superfluous. He is the first among many who follow in His footsteps. And He did it perfectly, and so He will forever be our ruler. Remember, when we—the few true believers—see Jesus again, we will be like Him, having moved from simply being a physical being to becoming a physical-spirit being, for lack of a better term. Jesus became who He became through the life He lived in the flesh and the fleshly death He freely died. We will become who we are to become by the life we live in the Spirit and the flesh we freely die to while still in this body. Christ took on our flesh. We take on His Spirit. That is what this is all about!

All of creation, all of life, all of time, all the pain, suffering, temptation, and self-denial are for this end and this end alone. To create a tree, an elephant, a planet, or maybe even an angel, God can simply speak the thing into existence. However, it would seem that to create a man into the very image of God is not done in an instant. Becoming human happens without our choosing, and that can be instantaneous (conception). But to become a righteous, godly, holy person, capable of fellowship with our righteous Creator for eternity, requires our free will to choose—or not to choose. These choices happen over the passage of time. It is not a one-time event but daily decisions made in the face of a lifetime of temptations, just like Jesus, our example. It is suffering, pruning, and refining that produce a righteousness that cannot be accomplished in a two-minute prayer. Even Jesus could not get around it. It is why God allowed Satan to tempt His own Son, mock Him, humiliate Him, slander Him, and eventually torture Him. Again, remember, it was the Holy Spirit who led Jesus to Satan for this purpose. Jesus came to show us what it will take in this life to be conformed into the physical-spirit beings who will walk with God for eternity. God Himself is not evil, and in Him no evil exists, but all creation—including both good and evil angels, good and evil men, and even animals—are at His disposal to produce the outcome He desires. Yes, even the acts of sinful men and angels are called upon, and Satan is only happy to comply.

Think of the story of Joseph. What Joseph's brothers meant for evil, God allowed and meant for ultimate good. So, when you believe Satan is coming at you with evil intent, know that you are being tested by God Himself, just as Joseph was in the prisons he ended up in, through no fault of his own. He had to pass that test, and he did. Your job is to pass that test as well: to flee from temptation, to deny your flesh, to not get angry and lash out, to not turn from God, to not entertain lustful thoughts. It's to go the extra mile, to give from your poverty, to love the unlovable, and so on. It may be your chance at turning the other cheek or swallowing your pride and allowing yourself to be cheated. These tests, and more importantly, how you come through them, are what will determine where you spend eternity—not Satan, and not some one-time moment of earnest faith. Moving on.

So, who actually is considered to be converted or "saved"? Exactly how and when does that take place? Can we even know?

"Now when the apostles who were in Jerusalem (one city) *heard that those in* Samaria (another city) **had received the Word of God,** *they sent Peter and John to them, who, when they had come down,* **prayed for them that they might receive the Holy Spirit.** *For as yet He had fallen on none of them.* **They had only been baptized in the name of the Lord Jesus."** (Acts 8:14-16 NKJV)

In this account from Acts 8, do you consider these Samaritans saved after they received the Word of God and were baptized? The modern church wants desperately to believe that belief (that is, belief, in and of itself) is the only requirement for eternal salvation. If this is correct, were these Samaritans considered saved and/or forgiven after they "received the Word of God" but before they were baptized? (I assume "received" means heard and believed the truth of it.) If your answer is yes, then what does Peter mean in Acts 2 when he says, "Repent and be baptized in the name of Jesus Christ for the forgiveness of sins"? Were these new believers forgiven simply because they believed the gospel? Or, after coming to believe, in order to be forgiven, did they need to repent and/or be baptized first, as Peter commands here? But wait, then we see that these Samaritans weren't actually filled with the Holy Spirit until sometime later when Peter and John came into town. Since we know that to enter the kingdom of heaven one must be filled with the Holy Spirit, at what point exactly do we consider those in Samaria to have been saved? I don't know how long it took to get the word from Samaria to Peter and John in Jerusalem, and then for them to travel back to Samaria (about 45 miles each way), but I'm pretty sure it didn't all happen the same day. It could have taken a week or even a month. Scripture doesn't tell us. Word and travel happened slowly back then compared to today. Did Peter and John drop everything they were doing and rush to Samaria? We're not told. So, we can't know. So, stop guessing.

In Acts 5, we are told the Holy Spirit is given to those who are obedient to Christ.

"And we are witnesses to these things, and so also is the Holy Spirit whom God has given to those who obey Him." (Acts 5:32 NKJV)

In Acts 10, Peter states,

*"But in every nation, whoever **fears Him** _and_ **works righteousness** is accepted by Him."* (Acts 10:34 NKJV)

Here, Scripture says that in order to be accepted by Christ, we must obey Him, fear Him, and do works of righteousness. This is getting complicated! And what of repentance? Where is its place in all of this? Scripture teaches that it is also required. Mustn't that take place in order to be born again? How can you be born to one until you die to the other, correct?

"Repent and be baptized, every one of you, in the name of Jesus Christ for the forgiveness of your sins, and you will receive the gift of the Holy Spirit." (Acts 2:38 ESV)

It seems as though there is no particular order or formula that must take place for one to come to "saving" faith in Christ. It can only be that God knows exactly when someone has been born again, but maybe we can't! If this is true, if not for ourselves, then definitely not for someone else. How could we then tell another believer they've been "saved" at a particular point in time? Rather, isn't it the case that only time will tell?

Let's look at another occasion in Acts (chapter 10):

*"While Peter was still speaking these words, **the Holy Spirit fell upon all those who heard the word**... Then Peter answered, 'Can anyone forbid water, that these should not be baptized who have received the Holy Spirit just as we have?' **And he commanded them to be baptized in the name of the Lord...**"* (Acts 10:44-48, fragmented, NKJV)

While Peter is talking to a group of people, the Holy Spirit falls on those who "heard the word" (that is, heard it and believed it). It was then that they were filled with the Holy Spirit. It's after the Holy Spirit comes into them that Peter baptizes them. Notice, this is a different order of things than is recorded in chapter 8 with the people of Samaria. There, they were baptized first; here, it came last (and please notice that Peter baptized them without anyone having to take a baptism class first).

The truth is, much takes place when turning from one life (this world) to entering another (the kingdom of God). But shepherds who would come after grew impatient, so they devised a way to condense all that must take place into two minutes:

- Jesus, I believe in you. (check)
- I believe you lived a sinless life and died for me in order that I might live forever with you. (check)
- I am a sinner in need of a savior. (check)
- I repent of my old life. (check)
- I ask that you forgive me of all my past sins. (check)
- Please now fill me with your Holy Spirit. (check)
- In Jesus' name I pray. (check)
- "Now, everybody get in the water!" (check)

How presumptuous can you get? Now, many in the church believe one can't be saved unless he/she says the sinner's prayer! That is heresy! This has become one of many doctrines that man now practices as if it is a requirement for salvation, for entrance into the kingdom of God, or to be a member at their church—as if it is a biblical mandate. It isn't! Simply saying those things in a prayer doesn't at all mean they took place. Some are just verbal acknowledgements that may or may not have, in actuality, become a reality in the soul of the one repeating the prayer (take repentance, for instance). Other statements in that prayer are requests, but God is not obligated to say yes to our requests. Surely, many people say the sinner's prayer because they love someone close to them and are desiring to make them happy.

My point is this: It's awesome when people come to faith in Jesus. But not one of us knows what's going on inside a person's soul at that moment of acknowledging Christ as God. We can't know if they were born again at that very moment, or if that will come later for them—if ever. The Holy Spirit is invisible to the eye. The only way to know a person has been filled with the Spirit of Christ is by the life being lived. Going back to the parable of the Sower and the Seed, Jesus Himself claims they believed, so we can't say that they did not. But only one of the four received eternal salvation. And what was the proof, or assurance, of that? The bucket loads of fruit they produced in their lives!

Maybe it would help if we defined terms. What do you and I mean when we say someone has been "saved"? I believe many, if not most, hold that salvation happens once and that this one-time salvation occurs the moment someone comes to believe the gospel of Jesus Christ. I have come to believe that this is only true in part. There is indeed a salvation that comes when we have been forgiven of all of our sins committed before coming to faith in Christ and are filled with the Holy Spirit—our sinful self dying away along with our flesh—and at that point, starting to be transformed into our new self that was born in the Spirit. Had we not been born of the Spirit, we would have died in our flesh. But by grace, we were saved from our past lives through faith. This salvation is what I am calling "conversion salvation." This is salvation out of an evil world and from our fleshly selves and into the kingdom of God and our spiritual selves.

"And with many other words he testified and exhorted them, saying, 'Be saved from this perverse generation.'" (Acts 2:40 NKJV)

This verse does not read "be saved from hell" or "from eternal judgment." This "salvation" is from the world of darkness and into a world of light. This, however, should not be thought of as our only salvation moment.

Noah, along with his family of seven, was saved from the wrath of God upon the whole world. They were "saved from this perverse generation," referring to all the people of earth, but not necessarily from God's end times wrath that is still to come. Lot, his wife, and daughters received salvation from God's judgment against Sodom and Gomorrah. They were "saved from this perverse generation," referring to Sodom. Then, of course, the nation of Israel's crossing of the Red Sea was their salvation from Egypt, "this perverse generation."

In 1 Corinthians 10:11, Paul tells us that the accounts just mentioned were recorded specifically for us believers today, for our admonition, not for our comfort. The warning is that while salvation comes once to all who believe, there is a second salvation that is yet to be determined and only for those who remain steadfast in their obedience to the faith after being rescued from life in the world. That is why we are being warned! Otherwise, Paul's warning is pointless.

Christ saving Noah and his family from the life-ending flood in no way guaranteed them salvation unto eternal life with God. Each one of them was still required to walk with God after their initial salvation, after the ark came to rest. Don't you agree? If they didn't endure till the end and ended up in hell, it still would not have changed the fact that God saved them from the flood. Do we think they all are in heaven now? Think about the actions of Noah's son, Ham, while Noah was passed out in his tent. We then read in the account of Lot that his wife was killed by God within minutes of her salvation from the firestorm that rained down on Sodom. That incident was recorded for us as a warning. Her salvation didn't last long, did it? And what of Lot's incestuous daughters? Do we just assume that they will now escape the firestorm from the life-ending days of eternal judgment? Why? Their mother didn't. The salvation from the first didn't assure salvation from the second.

There is then, of course, the greatest example that eternal salvation is not a guarantee, coming from the most popular salvation account in the Bible: the salvation of Israel, a million people saved. Their Savior had come to set them free from bondage in order to bring them to the promised land. Out of all the adults saved from Egypt, only Caleb and Joshua were actually granted entrance by the Lord into the land He swore to give them. In all three of these examples, these pictures of "the way," it's evident that our initial salvation from life in the world (temporal) does not guarantee salvation from the second death (eternal). This faulty thinking is exactly what the Jews in the Bible mistakenly believed, and why Paul warns us not to make the same mistake in our thinking.

They heard God promise to give them that land, and so they assumed it was as good as there's, even though God made it so clear that His promises come with an "if".

Does this diminish our initial conversion salvation? Not at all! Those turning from their worldly living (repentance) are not only forgiven by the blood of Christ and set free from their slavery to sin (HALLELUJAH!), but because of this, they are then adopted into the family of God—now, not later! What a privilege! That alone is worth celebrating and glorifying God, since only those in the family of God will ever be allowed entrance into heaven! Most never even get adopted. We should each exclaim, "Thank you, Lord, for this rare opportunity. I won't let you down!" As stated earlier, our initial salvation is what gave us our solid foundation to start from. But a foundation, in and of itself, is worthless if we don't build on it. We, each one of us, were walking in a way that leads to death when God called us to repent, so we turned and came to Him. This conversion salvation is salvation from our very own hearts, from the slavery of our flesh. It is our conversion to God and kingdom living, away from this sinful world and its evil influences. God rescued Israel from the world and brought them out to be among themselves. Over time, however, they went back to living as they once did. Even their children, after eventually crossing over into Canaan, invited the world and its ways back in. All died because of these things. That's the lesson recorded for us. It's a warning so that we do not follow them!

But that's the first salvation. The second salvation is salvation from the fire of eternal hell and into the eternal kingdom of heaven. This then is our "eternal salvation." It comes with a new body, a new earth, and a new universe! And it is at this time, and only at this time, that the matter has been decided eternally. This is when we finally and eternally receive our rest. No longer will we have to be on guard from that evil Satan. No longer will we need to endure any temptations. No longer will sin be a thing we must run from. Fear? Gone. Worry? Gone. Death, pain, and danger? Gone. Eternally! Our eternal salvation.

Now, with this understanding, if when considering yourself or someone else "saved," you mean saved from a sinful life once lived, then I agree you can say you have been "saved." But still, you must allow time to prove that out. However, if by "saved" you mean you have been saved from the coming worldwide wrath of God and ultimately hell, you cannot say that, for that day has not yet come. You can fight vigorously for eternal salvation, as Jesus called us to do ("strive to enter"); you can pray for it before God, and you should. But until you experience it, until you are in your immortal body, you cannot claim to have obtained it already. Paul rightly did not.

"Not that I have already obtained this or am already perfect, but I press on to make it my own, because Christ Jesus has made me his own. Brothers, I do not consider that I have made it my own. But one thing I do: forgetting what lies behind and straining forward to what lies ahead, I press on toward the goal for the prize

of the upward call of God in Christ Jesus. Let those of us who are mature think this way." (Philippians 3:12-16 ESV)

*"Therefore, my beloved, as you have always obeyed, not as in my presence only, but now much more in my absence, **work out your own salvation** with fear and trembling."* (Philippians 2:12 ESV)

That is to say, because by God's grace you were saved from a life leading to death and then given an opportunity to live a new life in the ways of Christ, you must now work toward your own eternal salvation just as Paul did his. It is to be the ultimate goal in life—not just hoped for, and absolutely not just assumed, but fought for. Vigorously! That is what "striving" means! But too many in the church today believe because they recited some two-minute prayer that they need not strive after heaven anymore; that it's a sure thing, waiting for them because God has promised it to them—without understanding, as the stories I just mentioned show, that the promises of God come with an "if." They always have. They always will. Please consider this: We all know the unbeliever doesn't strive after heaven. Of course. But if after coming to faith in Christ, we who believe don't need to strive to that end, then who in the world is Christ speaking to when He tells us to "strive" to get in? My goodness, the entitlement mentality that so many in the church speak against in the West is alive and well, and in the Christian church itself, no less. Shameful. We are entitled to absolutely nothing. Nothing. "We are but unworthy servants, doing only what is our duty to do."

Are you getting it? The runner in the race, of whom Paul in the next passage is referring to, is not just assuming he will finish but is doing everything he can to make that a reality. He won't know for sure this is the case until he crosses the finish line—and not until then. And this is no fifty-yard dash either. This is a long-distance race. So, to the question, "Are you saved?" my response would be, "God saved me out of the sinful life I was living, and now I strive to one day be saved from His eternal judgment and into the eternal kingdom of heaven."

We now, as mentors, are to come alongside those who profess their new faith in Christ, those saved by the grace of God, and walk with them. We are to love them as brothers and sisters in the Lord, but let's also allow them to race for the goal of the prize and not assure them that their eternal reward is already there waiting no matter how they run the race.

"Do you not know that those who run in a race all run, but one receives the prize? Run in such a way that you may obtain it (why would he tell us this if we already have it?). *And everyone who competes for the prize is temperate in all things. Now they* (the natural/fleshy man) *do it to obtain a perishable crown, but we* (the spiritual man) *for an imperishable crown* (that's the goal!). *Therefore, I run* (verb) *thus: not with uncertainty. Thus, I fight* (verb): *not as one who beats the air. But **I discipline my body and bring it into subjection,** <u>lest,</u> when I have preached to others, **I myself should become disqualified.**"* (1 Corinthians 9:24-27 NKJV)

Why does Paul bring his body into subjection, meaning he disciplines it and denies his flesh? He willingly endures all of those things in his Christian walk, he says, lest he himself should become disqualified from finishing the race, after he was so graciously allowed to enter the race. And he surely is saying if he doesn't finish, he too will be denied that imperishable reward—heaven. To come to any other understanding is to purposely turn a blind eye to what Scripture is so obviously teaching.

So, what about you? Have you been living your life under a false assumption that because you once said "the sinner's prayer," you are guaranteed an eternal reward whether you finish or not? Whether you compete by the rules or not? It's critical that you get this right. We have listened to too many voices telling us a lie about salvation.

Throughout this book, I have been making arguments for cutting out so many voices of influence in our lives. I believe they are distractions from the One Voice we are to be spending the bulk of our lives listening to. In fact, God says we are to be in His voice daily! In the last chapter, I will be speaking about the voices of counsel that I believe too many in the church lean on in order to "fix" their lives here in this world.

CHRISTIAN COUNSELING

"One thing I do: forgetting what lies behind and straining forward to what lies ahead, I press on toward the goal for the prize of the upward call of God in Christ Jesus... Let those of us who are mature think this way, and if in anything you think otherwise, God will reveal that also to you." (Philippians 3:13-15, ESV)

Speaking of too many voices (uh-oh, here I go again), most pay-by-the-hour Christian counseling is unnecessary and/or useless, in my opinion.

*"Come, all you who are thirsty, come to the waters; and **you who have no money,** come, buy and eat! Come, buy wine and milk **without money** and without cost. Listen, **listen to me,** and **eat what is good,** and your soul will delight in the richest of fare."* (Isaiah 55:1-2, NIV)

Are you trying to bring delight to your soul? God's prescription for that is listening to Him. He is our great Counselor, and He wants to be! And He charges nothing for His sessions.

*"It is better to trust in **the Lord** than to put confidence **in man**."* (Psalm 118:8, NKJV)

*"**Your** testimonies are my counselors."* (Psalm 119:24, NKJV)

*"**The Lord of hosts** is wonderful in counsel and excellent in guidance."* (Isaiah 28:29, NKJV)

*"**All Scripture** is given by inspiration of God and **is profitable** for doctrine, for reproof, for correction, for instruction in righteousness, so that the man of God may be complete, thoroughly equipped for every good work."* (2 Timothy 3:16-17, NKJV)

*"With **Him** are wisdom and strength, He has counsel and understanding. With **Him** are strength and prudence."* (Job 12:13,16, NKJV)

It seems to me that God feels pretty confident the answers you seek to the problems you have are most likely findable in His Word. Here in the United States, we have thousands of professional "Christian counselors" available to us now that we didn't have even 50 years ago. I'm curious— with all this pay-by-the-hour counseling we afford ourselves these days, is the divorce rate (and remarriage, which is even more sinful than divorce) among Christians lower or higher than it was a hundred or two hundred years ago? How about the suicide rate? How about alcohol or drug addictions? Is fornication on the decline in the church? With all of the "expert" Christian counseling available to us today, shouldn't all these things be in great decline? Hmmm?

In effect, although they would never come right out and say it, too many in the church believe the Christian counseling industry itself is "given by inspiration of God" and is "profitable for doctrine, for reproof, for correction, for instruction in righteousness, that the man of God may be complete, thoroughly equipped for every good work."

Just like the influence the world has on the church and her love affair with Christian Bible colleges and seminaries, if the world says the professional counseling industry is important, the church believes it must be. Today, Christians have over 200,000 Christian counselors available to them in the United States alone.

Counseling is deemed so important among Christians that, so often, it is the first suggestion given to anyone who is hurting. I know it was the case in my own life. When I was dealing with an ending marriage, my friends started suggesting "good" counselors they knew of. I went to my church pastor for advice, and he too gave me a list of recommended counselors. In all of my troubles and all my dealings with pastors (plural) and counselors (plural), not one of them asked me how well I knew the Bible. Outrageous! How could God's counsel, God's only holy and spiritual Word, not be the "go-to"?

Both counselors, on the first day I met with them, suggested their favorite books on what I was going through. What should have happened is that each shepherd—pastor or counselor—should have handed me a Bible and said, "Go read this. And keep reading it. The answers you seek to the problems you have are all between the covers of this book." But they didn't, because they didn't believe it themselves. As they see it, when in trouble, turn to "a professional," or another book. Sad indeed.

Had I sat in counseling sessions for years, I would still be nowhere near where I have come, sitting at the feet of God's great counsel, given to me by God Himself. Because of His mighty counsel, this Christian man is walking a 180 in his life—not just in one single aspect, but in almost all! No psychology, no techniques, no "how does it make you feel?" No, "How can we change your circumstance?" And absolutely no excuses or pardons. And all for the one-time purchase price of a Bible.

If a Christian has a problem they are struggling with in their lives, the church's answer is counseling. "Marriage problem? Drinking problem? Parenting problem? Depression? For just $150 per session, we're nearby and we're here to help." Don't you see? That's the world's answer as well! Is there no power in Christ? Is today's world and its problems too sophisticated for God to handle? He is God! If He can't help the lost and the hurting because of the complicated world in which we now live, what a weak god our God has turned out to be. Created the entire universe? Yes. Raised people from the dead? Yes. Fix a struggling marriage today, or your constant need to feel wanted and respected? Probably not. But that's not true. God, our great Counselor, is the answer for what ails the believer—not some college-educated, paid-by-the-hour, makes-more-money-the-more-hours-he/she-spends-with-you therapist.

Hear this: I feel the need to repeat this truth a lot—God is His word, and His word is God. They are, in so many instances, interchangeable. Let's see if God believes His words are the words you need to hear:

• *"It is better to trust in the words of God than to put confidence in man."* • *"The words of God are my counselors."* • *"The words of God are wonderful in counsel and excellent in guidance."* • *"With the words of God are wisdom and strength; His words are my counsel and understanding. With His words come strength and prudence."*

But instead, what do those in the church of Christ tell people "struggling" with issues in their lives? Answer: "I feel terrible about your struggle. I know you're hurting. Here's the business card of someone who can help." Good grief. Even the professed Christian has bought into the lie that you must be "professionally" trained in order to counsel someone well. You're supposed to be a Christian, Christian! You yourself are to know the biblical concepts of God, and so you should be able to guide your troubled friends and loved ones with biblical principles, wisdom, and discernment.

Most need counseling because they do not know the Word of God and, most importantly, they haven't been in the habit of living in obedience to it or putting its concepts and precepts into practice. It is a practice, a lifestyle, that takes years of commitment and striving. This path is what brings contentment, peace, hope, and delight to the soul. But it absolutely does not happen overnight. Too many Christians don't want anything to do with this lifestyle that God prescribes, yet they still want the peace and joy He promises in their lives. But it doesn't work that way.

So many are just looking for someone to make their pain or problems go away. And I guess if that's the case, maybe a counselor is a good idea, because God didn't come to take our problems and pain away, that's for sure. It is through our pain that He does His best work!

"Therefore we do not lose heart, but though our outer person is decaying, yet our inner person is being renewed day by day. ***For our momentary, light affliction is producing for us an eternal weight of glory far beyond all comparison,*** *while we look* **not** *at the things which are seen, but at the things which are not seen; for the things which are seen are temporal, but the things which are not seen are eternal."* (2 Corinthians 4:16-18, NASB)

Counselors are a self-selected group. They surely love what they do. And they should, it's right up their alley—not in that they know people better than others, but in that they love to hear people's darker side and give advice. Now that I think about it, I should have been a counselor! And, of course, so many don't live by the counsel they give, you understand, but they sure do love to give it. And this doesn't seem to bother them.

"Take the log out of your own eye, ***and then*** *you can see clearly to take the speck out of your brother's eye."* (Matthew 7:5, ESV)

"I will not dare to speak of any of those things that Christ has not accomplished through me, in word and deed, to make Gentiles obedient." (Romans 15:18, NKJV)

These therapists counsel with advice they themselves do not follow. I do not have respect for the industry as a whole, and counseling done in the name of Jesus ranks even lower. I've met my share of therapists over 35 years in sales and have been perplexed at their "wisdom." I often walk away thinking, "People pay you for your counsel?" You see, just like the problem with who will pastor a church, it's not the character and wisdom given by God Himself through the study of His own words that determine who is qualified to counsel a soul, but rather a degree, a certificate, or what it really is—a receipt. And, like many of you no doubt, I have known many people who have spent lots of money on sessions and are no better off than they were before going in. They are poorer for it, however.

There are too many variables that are not taken into account that will always keep counseling from doing any good except to the counselor's bank accounts and egos. People, including so many professed Christians, are living in and for the flesh. There is no help for a Christian living this way. In fact, most personal issues believers struggle with are because they are not living by the Spirit of God within them, as required, but rather in the self-centeredness of their flesh—a flesh they were supposed to have died to when they were born again into the Spirit of Christ.

*"For the love of Christ controls us, because we have concluded this: that one has died for all, **therefore all have died**; and He died for all, (**so**)**that those who live might no longer live for themselves** but for Him who for their sake died and was raised."* (2 Corinthians 5:14-15, ESV)

Until you come to grips with this hard truth, you will always be discontented. But is a counselor going to tell their clients that? Not very likely. I'm not saying none of them do, but I am very skeptical that this is the norm. And are the counselors themselves living by this principle while counseling others to do it?

God's Word is for the spiritual believer, not the natural one. It works, it heals, it transforms like no counseling session can—but only to those dying to themselves and their desires, and striving to live according to God's instructions and principles. And yes, this often includes the victim-counselee. But dying and giving up the need for fairness, for instance, is too great a task that many have no true interest in tackling in their lives. And so, they will never be better off because of counseling sessions with a man. They need counseling from God, and they must be willing to heed His good counsel, or it is all in vain. If they won't hear—and more importantly, heed—God's good counsel, none of man's counsel will help them spiritually. And if they haven't grown spiritually from counseling, then the entire time spent in sessions was wasted, for spiritual growth is the only growth that should matter to the Christian—it is the only growth that is eternal.

On a practical level, people lie to counselors. Couples lie. Their perspectives are slanted, they give half-truths, their memories are faulty, and they often do not even know themselves. They make up emotions and come to conclusions based on faulty knowledge of themselves and on an unbiblical view of what their lives are supposed to look like as Christians. So often, they may not even be that committed to the process that the counselor is trying to lead them through. And this goes for both individuals and couples.

To get people totally sold out to becoming who they must become in order for their lives or marriages to work is rare indeed. They break down in tears during a session, and their therapist thinks, or says, "I think we've made a breakthrough today." Please. Tears are an indicator of no such thing.

It is my opinion that so often Christian/biblical counselors do not know the very Bible they profess to be counseling from. They know things that are in the Bible, but they haven't a clue as to what these precepts are truly teaching or what the overall message of the life Scripture prescribes. And yet, they presume to lead in "biblical" concepts?

These Christian counselors don't pour into Scripture, but rather they pour into books and studies on human psychology. They then try to counsel the flesh of a person—but the flesh is sinful and will always be such. The flesh can never truly be at peace because it constantly requires pleasure, or a feeling of acceptance, or respect to get there. But, of course, these things are never promised, nor does Scripture ever teach that they are necessary for the true believer to feel contentment. In fact, the desire for these is the very poison that kills the spirit in a man. These are spiritual truths, but they are not accepted as such, not in the world of psychology. Human psychology is another term for "the flesh." Don't you see? The study of human psychology is the study of the mind of man, not the mind of Christ—which is the very mind that we are supposed to have as believers!

The person who is a Christian counselor, but not filled with the Spirit of God—which I believe is most of them—cannot speak to another's spirit; they can only speak to the flesh. And on top of that, if they do try to counsel in an attempt to bring peace to the spirit, but with ideas and concepts that only can bring peace to the flesh (the human psyche), they can never succeed because the spirit and the flesh can never live in harmony. If the flesh of a Christian man ever becomes somehow at peace, it can happen only at the death of the spirit in the man. And the reverse is also true.

To counsel the spirit, all counsel and principles must come from the Word of God, for it is the only word that can reach and transform a spiritual man. On the other hand, biblical precepts and concepts cannot be lived out in the flesh and bring peace from within. These two worlds are at odds with each other. It does no good to appease the flesh, for to do so inevitably brings selfishness, as the flesh is self-seeking. It's why so many people are depressed—because they cannot take the focus of their lives off of themselves. And no, I'm not saying there aren't any wiring issues that can cause depression or anxiety. But we all have issues like that. And those won't ever leave until we get our new bodies. Not all, but most issues of unhappy Christians arise from a focus on oneself instead of a focus on the will or ways of God.

Is your marriage in decay? At least one of you is in the practice of sinning. Do you have a drinking problem? There are no excuses for it. Stop drinking. Problem with porn? This does not need to be discussed. It is sin. Put it away! Attracted to people of the same sex? Blame whoever you like, but God will condemn you if you act on it. The "why's" are not important.

To the world of psychology, the "why's" are important, but not to God. To the therapist, it is important to know how someone feels about something they are dealing with or have dealt with in the past. But, in the kingdom of God, God never asks about our feelings because our feelings are never considered by God to determine how He would have us live or judge another. Only the Word of God determines that, and it is the same for everyone. For instance, if someone slaps me on the cheek (insults me, embarrasses me, etc.), I am to "turn to him the other cheek." That is what it is to be a spiritual man. My feelings do not get a say. "Stick up for yourself" is not a spiritual precept, it's a worldly/fleshly one.

These days, the world/flesh desires others to know our "love language." But the spiritual Christian is only to be concerned with God's love language—what makes *Him* happy. The flesh wants to figure out ways to make itself happy, and it wants others to know that "way." But as spiritual believers, our feelings don't play a role in how we are to live. It only matters how God feels about how we are to live.

Nowhere in Scripture does God ask anyone why they felt led to sin or what they thought of His commands or precepts. Remember when Cain was mad because God accepted his brother Abel's offering of meat but not Cain's offering of fruit? Did our loving and compassionate God respond, "I'm sorry. Do you feel less worthy because I prefer your brother's offering? Did I hurt your heart in some way?" No! He basically says, "This is My preference, and you had better get with the program."

It doesn't matter how we feel! God is impartial. It doesn't matter how one ever came to be such an abusive husband or father. It does not matter if I ever come to understand why I became enslaved by porn before I repented of my old life. Why don't you feel loved and respected by others? Answer: It doesn't matter. As a follower of Christ, from this day forward, it only matters who the Word of God has called you to be today. Read it, do it, be it. So much of the rest is psychobabble.

*"Therefore, if anyone is in Christ, he is a **new** creature; **the old things passed away**; behold, new things have come."* (2 Corinthians 5:17, ESV)

*"One thing I do: **forgetting** what lies behind and straining forward to what lies ahead, I press on toward the goal for the prize*

of the upward call of God in Christ Jesus. **Let those of us who are mature think this way."** (Philippians 3:13-15, ESV)

But the world says, "Lets rehash the old things. It will be good." For far too many, their past lives and/or past selves are getting in the way of their obedience from here on out. That person from the past died with Christ. Stop visiting the dead. They're dead!

"Let me first understand why I am making these bad choices, or why I feel so unloved and unworthy, and if I do come to understand, then maybe I can get past it. Then maybe I can start feeling valuable again."

To "deal" with your past should not be about discussing it and rehashing all the feelings those incidents or seasons caused; rather, it should be about forgetting it. That's how Christians deal with their past. They simply leave it behind. You want God to forget your past, but you and your counselors want to keep bringing it up!

"As they were going along the road, someone said to Him, 'I will follow You wherever You go.' And Jesus said to him, 'Foxes have holes, and birds of the air have nests, but the Son of Man has nowhere to lay His head.' (Meaning, 'This ain't no joy ride.') To another He said, 'Follow Me.' But he said, 'Lord, let me first go and bury my father.' And Jesus said to him, 'Leave the dead to bury their own dead. But as for you, go and proclaim the kingdom of God.' Yet another said, 'I will follow you, Lord, but let me first say farewell to those at my home.' Jesus said to him, 'No one who puts his hand to the plow and looks back is fit for the kingdom of God.'" (Luke 9:57-62, ESV)

The principle here is that once Christ has called you, you're His—right now. You are to follow Him right now. Those issues from your past life are not your concern anymore, unless it's going back and righting the wrongs you yourself did. We should never leave those in the past. When possible, righting your wrongs is part of the *repentance* you were called to when Christ called you to Himself. And often, it's much more than "sorry." You must try to repay for the wrong you did.

*"But Zaccheus stopped and said to the Lord, 'Behold, Lord, half of my possessions I am giving to the poor, **and if I have extorted anything from anyone, I am giving back four times as much.'** And Jesus said to him, **'Today salvation has come to this house**, because he too is a child of Abraham.'"* (Luke 19:8-9, NASB)

But I digress.

May a particular issue someone is dealing with be more difficult to overcome for one person than for another? Of course! But the degree of difficulty doesn't change the command or the concept. The particular circumstances of your past may matter to people, but they don't matter to God. From this day forward, you are to put it all behind you and follow Him. And you'd better learn what "following Him" really means.

Someone who earns $10,000 a year may understandably be much more tempted to steal while in a store than someone who makes $100,000 a year, but the degree and frequency of temptation doesn't void God's law not to steal. Don't steal—whoever you are. Period. End of story. God says to divorce a spouse for any reason but infidelity is sinful. God also says if a divorced person, who is divorced for any reason other than an unfaithful spouse, remarries, they are committing adultery. And anyone who marries the divorced person commits adultery. A mean wife, or a falling-down-drunk wife, both fall into the "any" category. So, these divorces and remarriages are sinful, no matter the circumstances surrounding them.

"Hey Quinn, my husband leaves for days at a time. Many times, he doesn't even contact me while he's gone." Answer: That's in the "for any reason" file. So, God says you can't divorce him.

"My wife lies and belittles me all the time!" Answer: That's an "any" reason.

"My husband never comes to church with me. In fact, he's even admitted he doesn't believe in Christ." Answer: I'm so sorry, but that's also part of the "any" category.

"I feel completely alone in my marriage." Answer: That is a miserable way to go through life. God knows your pain. I hurt for you. I know the feeling myself of being completely alone. So, I have great sympathy for you. But you still must walk in obedience to God. If He wants you out of that situation, *He* will get you out—in His way— and in His timing. But you have to trust Him. You have to wait on Him, even if the waiting comes with pain and suffering in the meantime.

Surely Scripture teaches this—and not just about marriage. Read Peter. But that's a difficult concept to tell the hurting, isn't it? They just want the pain to stop, and we all understand that, especially those who have shared in the same type of suffering.

All the scenarios I just mentioned are undoubtedly crushing to the heart of the victim-spouse. I have personally heard dozens of these stories. What a sad and terrible way to have to live. But what I'm obviously getting at is that, to God, our feelings, past, or current afflictions aren't taken into account as to whether His laws can be broken or whether we have an excuse for who we are and how we behave. He simply states who we are to be now and how we are to live, and He commands that we fall in line. And so, now we're all on the same playing field because no one has an acceptable excuse. And so, now there's a lot less to figure out. And so, now there's a lot less counseling that needs to be done.

I've personally studied the divorce and remarriage subject extensively and do believe I understand why divorce and remarriage are forbidden. However, it truly doesn't matter if I understand why or not. God declares it, and that is that! So, to an individual or a couple who comes in for counseling because one or both are considering divorce, the only counsel is "You can't." How long could that take? Scripture tells you what is required of both of you. You will either comply or not. But your excuses are just that, excuses. If you divorce your spouse, you'll be sinning. It's that simple. If you remarry, you'll be committing adultery. It doesn't matter how either of you feels about it, or how bad you may be suffering. I've had plenty of Christian women tell me they felt like they had no other choice but to divorce because of the abuse they were suffering. To which I feel it fair to ask, "And what great injustice forced you to remarry?" Divorce is sinful, yes, but it's not adultery. It's remarriage that God considers adultery, and yet I've never heard a story of Christians feeling forced to remarry under duress. But I digress.

While married, you, husband, must behave in a manner toward your wife as prescribed by God through Scripture. Scripture lists no conditions based on her actions or your lack of feelings toward her that will void this command. Go do it. And you, wife, must also behave toward your husband as prescribed by God—and not only if he does his part. My individual counsel to either or both of you is to go live in obedience to God and let the chips fall where they may. God will do the rest.

*"Beware lest anyone cheat you through philosophy and empty deceit, **according to the tradition of men**, according to the **basic principles of the world**, and **not** according to Christ."* (Colossians 2:8, NKJV)

According Christ, the savior you profess to follow, divorce and remarriage are forbidden, with only one exception. Now, it's understandable that mankind views this as foolishness. But one look at the church of Christ and it's obvious that His followers are no more impressed with His commands than those of the world.

The counsel of Christ is, "Come die as I died, and live as I lived." Anything else for the Christian will be unfulfilling. But that type of counsel doesn't pay the bills, does it, counselor?

*"Make them bear their guilt, O God; **Let them fall by their own counsels;** Because of the abundance of their transgressions cast them out, **For they have rebelled against you**."* (Psalm 5:10, ESV)

*"Woe to the rebellious children, saith the LORD, that take counsel, **but not of Me**; and that cover with a covering, but not of My Spirit, **that they may add sin to sin**."* (Isaiah 30:1, KJV)

Okay, I've said enough. I'm not saying all counseling is wrong or bad. Yes, some people have no one to pour their heart out to, and a humble, compassionate counselor can help lighten the load. And no, there isn't anything wrong with having a good cry now and then or having someone honestly tell you they understand your pain. My sister recently told me, "Quinn, you're an honest and godly man. But you can be too direct sometimes. Maybe a little softness in your approach would be better in some situations." That type of counsel can be very productive as well. And yes, she is right, of course. But so much of counseling is unnecessary. My now-deceased brother-in-law was a pastor for 35 years, and during his counseling sessions, he sometimes had to say, "You're coming here for me to get you to do what you already know the Word of God has called you to do. Now, if God Himself can't get you to do it, what makes you think I can?" Exactly!

No doubt many counselors mean well, but they counsel with what they learned from books, classes, and other counselors—not from the implanted Word of God. And so, what good is it? The counselors who can most help the Spirit-filled believer are those who are experts in the Scriptures. The counsel of God is often more hard-hitting than people feel comfortable with. But we must give and receive the truth of God and His good counsel, or we will never become the people He has called us to be.

CLOSING

Recently, I saw this quote posted on social media:

"I don't go to church because I think I'm perfect. I go to church because I know I'm not."

Wake up! Church is not the source of our faith! Salvation is not found in church! But church has become a religion unto itself. As a body, we must agree to shut out all the voices that have taken over the church and become spokesmen for the church. Instead, we must give God's only holy, ordained Word our complete focus, to the exclusion of almost everything and everyone else.

Read the Bible just one time from beginning to end and see the pattern. You'll see I am right. Those who listened to the majority were always wrong. Those who listened only to the true words of God were rare and yet the only ones considered faithful to God by God. Come back to God. It is Christ who saves, not Christians. And Christ is the Word of God, the One Voice we are to follow.

I've been hard-hitting in this book. I know it may sound like I have a cold heart, but the lovely things of God—His compassion, grace, forgiveness, and mercy—can all be heard every Sunday or on almost any Christian podcast or read in most Christian books, often to the exclusion of concepts like the true fear of God, true repentance, obedience, hell, and the like. But those things are just as real and just as important in the life of a true follower of Christ. Proverbs 27:6 reads, "Faithful are the wounds of a friend, but deceitful are the kisses of an enemy."

I study the Scriptures and see these concepts and precepts, but I don't hear them taught with much conviction, and I don't see them lived out. So, I feel compelled to share the hard truths I believe aren't being heard. I love my brothers and sisters in Christ! And it's for that reason I'm willing to be, if need be, the bad guy, the scapegoat. I'm not comparing myself to the Apostle Paul, but I do feel like him when he asked, in effect, "Have I become your enemy because I feel burdened to tell you the hard truths?" I simply want everyone to know God because of, and through, God Himself.

That we have the Bible is a miracle in itself, and yet it seems to get so much less respect than it deserves. It is to be held above anything else in our lives. Christian authors get read, speakers get listened to, and podcasts get watched, but the Bible gets very little use in comparison. God's concepts, principles, moral codes, and difficult teachings are timeless and absolutely necessary, but the church has strayed far from many of them. We are, and will be, held just as much to account by them as any other time in the history of mankind. If you have read this entire book, you have been admonished, and I have done my duty of obedience.

May you walk in the light of Christ, abiding in Him, and He in you.

Printed in the United States
by Baker & Taylor Publisher Services

Printed in the United States
by Baker & Taylor Publisher Services